8/13

Ambition, Competition, and Electoral Reform

LEGISLATIVE POLITICS & POLICY MAKING

Series Editors

Janet M. Box-Steffensmeier, Vernal Riffe Professor of Political Science,
The Ohio State University

David Canon, Professor of Political Science, University of Wisconsin, Madison

Ambition, Competition, and Electoral Reform
The Politics of Congressional Elections Across Time

Jamie L. Carson and Jason M. Roberts

The University of Michigan Press
Ann Arbor

Published in the United States of America by
The University of Michigan Press
Manufactured in the United States of America
⊗ Printed on acid-free paper

2016   2015   2014   2013   4   3   2   1

A CIP catalog record for this book is available from the British Library.

ISBN 978-0-472-11864-9 (cloth : alk. paper)
ISBN 978-0-472-02895-5 (e-book)

Carson would like to dedicate this book to his Mom and Dad for their love and support over the years.

Roberts would like to dedicate this book to Steve Roberds and Steve Smith.

Contents

List of Tables

List of Figures

Acknowledgments

This book has been a work in progress for several—perhaps too many—
years. We were both still in graduate school when we started kicking
around the idea of writing a book on nineteenth and early twentieth
century House elections. Given that most research on congressional
elections we had encountered started with the 1946 elections (the
beginning of Gary Jacobson's data set on U.S. House elections), we
wondered whether many of the patterns we regularly observed in the
contemporary era with respect to congressional elections would extend
back further in time. For instance, have ambitious politicians always
behaved strategically or is this largely a function of entry and exit
decisions in a largely candidate-centered era? To what extent has
the decline in competitiveness of House elections across time been a
function of changing dynamics in candidate and partisan behavior? To
what extent did strong party organizations promote higher levels of
electoral competition during the late nineteenth century when control
over the nomination process was more exclusive? What effect did
changing electoral institutions such as the adoption of the Australian
ballot and direct primaries around the turn of the century have on
candidate emergence patterns? Have incumbents always been elected at
relatively high rates or has this pattern clearly become more prominent
over the last century? These and many other related questions are
what initially motivated our early discussions about this book.

During the writing process, the focus of our book steadily evolved
based on our changing interests, the comments and feedback of others,
and the availability of historical data. Collecting the historical House
elections data set that we employ for all the analysis in the book took
much longer than either of us originally and naively anticipated. Some
of the electoral return data we needed had previously been coded

electronically, but we had to fill in the gaps and correct numerous errors that we came across. Without a doubt, the most time consuming venture involved coding candidate experience across time. For this, we are especially indebted to a number of undergraduate and graduate students who assisted us with this effort. In particular, we would like to thank Dana Adams, Caitlin Dwyer, Matthew Holleque, Rob Holahan, Yagmur Sen, Justin Wedeking, and Matthew Weidenfeld. We also owe a special debt of gratitude to Lawrence Kestenbaum for updating and maintaining the Political Graveyard website and database, which was especially useful for tracking down unique biographical information on a number of candidates who ran for a seat in the U.S. House of Representatives.

The writing of two political scientists in particular has heavily influenced our combined interest in the study of congressional elections. First, David Mayhew's classic book, *Congress: The Electoral Connection*, has had an enormous impact on the way we view legislative behavior more generally, and members of Congress in particular. His simple argument about viewing legislators as "single-minded seekers of reelection" has stimulated an enormous amount of ideas and research on which we have both attempted to build to date. Second, we were both heavily influenced by Gary Jacobson's analysis in various editions of *The Politics of Congressional Elections*. This book in particular played a pivotal role in our decision to write our own book on House elections as it covered a number of different facets of electoral politics that encouraged us to think about congressional elections across time in new and innovative ways.

Roberts would like to thank Steve Roberds for first exposing him to congressional elections research and encouraging him to pursue a career in political science rather than the high school classroom. He is also deeply indebted to Steve Smith for being an energetic, compassionate, generous, and encouraging advisor and mentor. He would also like to thank Sarah Treul for her love, support, and the life/work balance she provided during the writing process. Carson would like to thank his PhD advisor and mentor, David Rohde, for introducing him to a broader understanding of Congress that served to reinforce his interest in congressional elections. He is also indebted to Jeff Jenkins, who first introduced him to historical research on congressional elections and American Political Development. Carson would also like to thank one of his undergraduate professors, Aimee Shouse, for initially introducing him to the exciting study of Congress and congressional elections.

We have presented parts of the book at various venues over the years. We are especially thankful to John Aldrich and David Rohde, both at Duke University, who allowed us to present an early version of our book at the weeklong Political Institutions and Public Choice (PIPC) Spring Book Seminar. Each year, John and Dave invite authors with a completed book manuscript to present their work in front of both faculty and graduate students to receive comments and critical feedback. The book is significantly better as a result of their helpful comments, ideas, and suggestions. We are also indebted to Erik Engstrom, Mike Brady, Brendan Nyhan, Jill Rickershauser, Ian McDonald, Meredith Barthelemy, and Jerry Houff for their attendance and numerous comments during the PIPC seminar.

Based on presentations at conferences and invited seminars, we would like to thank a number of individuals including David Brady, Gerald Gamm, Shigeo Hirano, Jeff Jenkins, David Parker, Wendy Schiller, and Richard Bensel for their helpful comments and feedback. Carson would like to thank the faculty at Texas A&M University and the American Politics Workshop at the University of Chicago for the opportunity to present this research and for the stimulating discussions regarding the evidence presented in the book. Several of our colleagues have offered helpful advice on one or more chapters and they deserve our gratitude as well. In particular, we want to thank Scott Ainsworth, Anthony Bertelli, Charles Bullock III, Michael Crespin, Erik Engstrom, Tim Johnson, Anthony Madonna, Shawn Treier, Sarah Treul, and Keith Poole. We want to especially acknowledge Ben Bishin, who read and commented on the entire manuscript. His insights, as usual, were very much appreciated. Carson would like to thank the students in his American Political Development course for offering a number of helpful and encouraging comments regarding an earlier version of this manuscript. Jonathan Slapin graciously let us use his LaTeXcode to produce the formatting of the final manuscript, which saved us a tremendous amount of time during the final stages of the process. Melody Herr and Susan Cronin at the University of Michigan Press deserve special thanks for shepherding our manuscript through the review process as do the anonymous reviewers who pushed us to make the final product as strong as possible. We also appreciate the careful copyediting of the book performed by Andrea Olson and the thorough indexing by Carrie Eaves. In the end, the revised manuscript is significantly better as a result of their efforts.

Portions of chapter 6 previously appeared in Jamie L. Carson, Erik

J. Engstrom, and Jason M. Roberts, 2007, "Candidate Quality, the Personal Vote, and the Incumbency Advantage in Congress," *American Political Science Review*, 101: 289–301, and are reprinted here with the permission of Cambridge University Press.

We are grateful to the Everett Dirksen Center for the receipt of a Congressional Research Grant in 2003 that helped us collect some of the early data we utilized for our analysis of strategic candidate emergence in Chapter 5. Carson would like to thank the University of Georgia Research Foundation (UGARF) for providing summer money in 2005 to work on the early stages of this book project. Roberts would like to thank the University of Minnesotas Grant-in-Aid of research program for financial support.

1

Introduction

1.1 A Tale of Two Elections: 1874 and 1974

By almost any measure, the congressional elections of 1874 were disastrous for the Republican Party. While incumbent legislators of the president's party are often evaluated unfavorably during midterm elections, 1874 was a particularly devastating year for Republicans.[1] The party lost 96 seats and majority status in the House of Representatives for the first time since the end of the Civil War. After opening the 43rd (1873–1875) Congress with a healthy 203 to 88 seat margin over the Democrats, House Republicans in the 44th Congress (1875–1877) found themselves outnumbered 107 to 181 by Democrats.[2] The Republican losses were not confined to one state or specific region of the country, rather it was a nationwide route. In the Eastern states of Connecticut, Massachusetts, New Hampshire, New Jersey, Pennsylvania, and New York, for instance, Republicans lost 31 seats. In Illinois, Indiana, Michigan, Ohio, and Missouri, Republicans lost an additional 27 seats. Democrats completed the sweep in the former Confederate states, adding 27 seats in that region of the country as well.

The scale and dispersion of the Republican losses in 1874 have led many historians and observers to focus on the national determinants for the loss. The Panic of 1873 hit the United States in 1873, beginning a 5 year recession that produced bank failures, closure of the stock market for 10 days, wage depression, and an unemployment rate as high as 14 percent. As the recession set in, President Ulysses S. Grant and the Republican Congress received considerable blame for failing to enact policies that would ease the panic. Rather than support policies that would ease the recession, President Grant instead vetoed a bill that would have inflated the currency and he, along with congressional Republicans, continued to adhere to protectionists' tariff policies that inflated the price of goods in the United States. As a result of the serious economic downturn in the United States, one historian, Edward Stanwood (1903(II),186), labeled the 1874 election a "political revolution" against the Republican party and its policies. In addition, the Grant administration was saddled with numerous scandals surrounding the unethical activities of appointed officials (Stanwood 1903).

In many ways, the 1874 election was eerily similar to one that would occur 100 years later in 1974. Once again, Republicans were weighed down in a midterm election by a scandal-plagued president and poor economic conditions. The combination of the Watergate scandal and President Nixon's subsequent resignation in August of that year turned the public against the Republican party. Things only got worse as newly inaugurated President Ford decided to pardon former President Nixon, a decision which was met with derision throughout the country. At the same time, President Ford was presiding over an economy that was losing jobs and facing heightened inflation. Though there was no congressional majority for the Republicans to lose in 1974, they ended up losing 43 seats in the House of Representatives, four seats in the Senate, and numerous state legislative seats and governorships across the country. All told, it was a devastating loss for the Republicans that set back their chances of winning majority control of the chamber for another two decades and set the stage for them to ultimately lose the presidency in 1976.

Despite the poor electoral showing for Republicans in 1974, scholars to date have found virtually no evidence to suggest that voters *directly* punished Republican congressional candidates for the state of affairs in the country. In fact, Jacobson and Kernell (1983) argue that the 1974 midterm elections were not a referendum on Ford, Nixon, or Watergate at all, but rather reflected the differences in candidate quality in each House seat. In congressional districts throughout the country, quality Democratic candidates—defined as candidates who previously held elective office—defeated Republican incumbents and challengers who ran, but lacked the requisite electoral experience.

The adverse electoral environment did hurt Republicans and help Democrats in candidate recruitment, but the electoral effects were filtered through candidate quality. In other words, incumbent legislators were much more vulnerable in races where a quality challenger emerged to run against them. Democrats had an easier time recruiting quality candidates to run in 1974 as a result of the national mood, while Republicans struggled to both recruit quality candidates and stem the flow of incumbent retirements. As a result of the political circumstances, the Democrats captured 75 seats in the midterm elections and this large group of Democratic freshmen eventually came to be known as the "Watergate babies" given the unique circumstances surrounding their arrival on Capitol Hill.

The 1974 election highlights many aspects of what Jacobson and Kernell refer to as the *Strategic Politicians Theory*. They argue (1983, 16–17)

> The point ... for any theory of national conditions and electoral change is plain. The dominant components of the individual voting decision are the voter's opinions about the candidates running in the district. ...The voters focus[ed] upon the choices in front of them rather than upon broad national issues.

Strategic politicians assessing the political circumstances in 1974 carefully considered local and national conditions when deciding whether or not it would be a good year to run for a House seat. The combination of the large number of Republican incumbent retirements and the negative backlash against the Nixon and Ford administrations made it a particularly good year for Democratic candidates with previous electoral experience to emerge. In fact, 41 percent of Republican incumbents who sought reelection faced a quality Democratic challenger, while only 10 percent of Democratic incumbents faced a quality Republican. Thus, when voters went to the polls on election day in 1974, it should come as no surprise that they selected a larger than average class of freshmen Democratic representatives given the imbalance in candidate quality across the two parties.

In light of the preceding discussion, what can Jacobson and Kernell's argument about strategic politicians tell us about the Republicans' electoral debacle in 1874? Most historians and political scientists would say, nothing. The Strategic Politicians Theory, as well as most other contemporary theories of congressional elections, was constructed and designed specifically to explain modern-day elections (i.e. post World War II) within a largely candidate-centered era of politics. Indeed, this theoretical framework reflects a phenomenon which arose during the mid-twentieth century, in which congressional candidates came to be viewed as electoral entrepreneurs working toward their own election or reelection rather than through the party apparatus. As we detail more fully in Chapter 2, party organizations recruited candidates and shouldered much of the responsibility for conducting elections in the United States during the nineteenth century. Prior to the adoption of the Australian or secret ballot at the end of the nineteenth century, it was substantially more difficult for individual candidates to develop personal loyalty as voters were essentially voting for a party slate and not making office-by-office choices.[3] In fact, Jacobson (1989, 787) argues that in this party-centered era of politics, "the quality of individual candidates would be of small electoral consequence."

Nevertheless, if we look more closely at individual elections across the country, the 1874 election outcomes have more in common with modern-day House elections than the portrait typically painted by historians writing about these elections would suggest. Indeed, the "political revolution" that Stanwood wrote about was limited to Republicans facing a high quality challenger. Only 15 percent of Republican incumbents facing a quality challenger won in 1874 compared with 81 percent for those facing a non-quality challenger (i.e. those who had held previous elective office). This disparity in outcomes across candidate quality is not consistent with the notion that national tides alone swept Republicans out of office—as a matter of fact, it sounds more like the type of electoral result we would find during the contemporary era as noted above in reference to 1974. As the *The New York Times* noted in describing the loss of six Republican seats in Indiana:

> There were several really bad nominations. The candidacy of Benjamin F. Claypool, in the Sixth District, against William S. Helman, was especially unfortunate. Had the district been raked, a more unpopular man than Mr. Claypool could not easily have been found. His own county, Fayette, went against him. (*The New York Times*, October 24, 1874, 3)

Our data suggest the Indiana 6th was no aberration as only 14 percent of Democratic incumbents faced a quality challenger in 1874, compared to 47 percent of Republican incumbents.

Most accounts of elections during the late nineteenth and early twentieth centuries have focused almost exclusively on presidential contests at the top of the ticket. In fact, there is surprisingly little work that has focused more generally on congressional elections during this era. When congressional elections have received limited attention by historians writing about this era, the scholarly emphasis has largely been on aggregate party outcomes in Congress or dramatic swings in party control in election years such as 1864, 1882 or 1894 (Martis 1989). Unfortunately, little systematic attention has been given to explaining *why* such changes occurred from one election to the next or how strategic politicians may have been a factor in determining the outcome in individual elections.[4] In this book, we focus specifically on the important role played by candidates, parties, and institutional development on changes in electoral competition since the 1870s. In doing so, we correct misperceptions in how early congressional elections have been portrayed by scholars.

In structuring our discussion throughout the book, we think it is important to first provide a solid foundation of existing research on the subject of elections. As noted above, very little work has focused specifically on congressional elections during the late nineteenth and early twentieth centuries—what little research we did uncover is discussed in greater depth in Chapter 2. Following this discussion, we lay out our primary theoretical argument regarding strategic politicians and how we expect them to impact elections from this era. Even with strong parties regulating elections in this period, we maintain that both parties sought to recruit the most experienced candidates possible, which led to more competitive and closely fought races in many election years for our study. After presenting our theoretical framework in Chapter 3, we offer a voluminous amount of descriptive evidence in Chapter 4 before turning to more systematic analyses in the next two chapters. These three chapters are the heart of our empirical analysis and provide an extensive amount of previously unavailable evidence to draw upon in supporting our theoretical framework. We conclude with a summary of our findings and a broader discussion of the implications of our research with respect to accountability and representation in the electoral arena.

One of the central and underlying themes that runs throughout the ensuing chapters is that decisions among candidates and the party elite regarding the composition of the ballot (i.e. who was running and when) were a major determinant of election outcomes in the era between Reconstruction and the close of World War II. This runs contrary to the perception in the literature that individual candidates had little impact on election outcomes during this era. Through a comprehensive analysis of our newly collected elections data, we present evidence of how parties recruited strong candidates to run for office during the late nineteenth century and how this changed dramatically with the adoption of new institutions such as the Australian ballot and the direct primary in the early twentieth century. In this respect, we think that our findings will offer new insights about congressional elections and lead scholars to reevaluate the fit between existing theories and historical data. In short, we believe our findings demonstrate that the strategic choices by individual politicians have always played a large role in determining election outcomes.

1.2 Analyzing Congressional Elections

We believe the study of congressional elections is important for a number of different reasons. As the architect of the U.S. Constitution—James Madison—firmly believed, elections are the central mechanism that ensure popular sovereignty over the government. As the people's branch, members of Congress are supposed to listen to and be responsive to the interests of their constituents. If an incumbent legislator is doing a good job of representing her constituents and desires to be reelected, then there is a strong likelihood that she will continue to serve in Congress. If the incumbent fails to adequately represent her constituents, however, then regularly occurring elections provide voters with a chance to replace the "out-of-touch" legislator with someone else who promises to do a better job. Over time, and assuming the electoral machinery continues to work effectively, the cycle repeats itself and a new group of legislators continues to get elected by the voters.

Given the paramount importance of congressional elections in American democracy, we think it important that scholars have as complete an understanding of the changing nature of elections as is practicable. Historical studies are important in this regard, as Swift and Brady (1994, 95) note, "the breadth and depth of an historical perspective suggest a host of causal factors often too subtle or inchoate for contemporary observers to adequately grasp." Elections from an earlier era may be interesting in and of themselves, but we believe that studying them has even more to offer than simply uncovering a unique series of electoral events that occurred more than 100 years ago. In addition to providing a more complete account of American electoral development, we think an historical perspective provides us with a certain amount of analytical leverage.

Most importantly, the discussion in the subsequent chapters sheds light on how a central democratic mechanism (i.e., congressional elections) has evolved over time and both how and why this mechanism works the way that it does in the political system. In particular, the introduction of the Australian ballot at the end of the nineteenth century and the widespread adoption of the direct primary during the early part of the twentieth century are two of the most fundamental changes in American electoral institutions since the ratification of the U.S. Constitution in 1789. Both of these institutional changes had the effect of transferring control of the machinery of elections away from the party organizations and toward the states and voters. To date, we lack a systematic analysis that evaluates the effects of these institutional changes on congressional elections over time. Studying elections before, during, and after these fundamental changes allows us to examine their effects on candidates, parties, and electoral outcomes. Moreover, it provides an opportunity to systematically evaluate the role that strategic politicians played in influencing congressional elections across time.

As we noted above, modern theories of congressional elections have not been tested with pre–World War II data to determine if they are equally relevant across a longer time span. In doing this, we are the first to test these theories with out-of-sample data. This allows us to assess the applicability of these theories in this historical context and to test the central assumptions made with modern data. For instance, many theories of candidate entry decisions assume that candidate-centered elections are a necessary condition for evidence of strategic behavior and a "personal vote" connection with voters. We show in Chapter 5 that many elements of the strategic politicians theory proposed by Jacobson and Kernell (1983) are applicable in a party-centered era. Likewise, we demonstrate that an incumbency advantage has existed since Reconstruction and that our time series gives us leverage in assessing the applicability of a variety of potential explanations for this trend. Moreover, it is the variability in electoral competition and institutions that offers us considerable leverage in understanding how electoral outcomes have changed over time.

The current state of congressional elections in the United States has led many people to question the ability of electoral institutions to produce democratic responsiveness. Despite low approval ratings, the composition of Congress changes very little. More than 90 percent of incumbents routinely seek and gain reelection—often by large margins—and very few seats are considered "competitive" in any given election. In contrast, during the late nineteenth century, it was not unusual for approximately half of all winning candidates to receive less than 55 percent of the vote in congressional races. However, by the 1920s, less than 20 percent of congressional elections were decided by such a narrow margin, suggesting a substantial decline in electoral competitiveness over time. Given the obvious connection between the decline in competitiveness and electoral responsiveness, we investigate this relationship more systematically in this book. Indeed, we present some preliminary evidence in Chapter 4 documenting this trend over time. Then, we turn to more systematic evidence in Chapter 5 suggesting that the waning role of political parties in the nomination process is at least partly to blame for the decline of electoral competition in the twentieth and into the twenty-first century.

Recent years have witnessed a dramatic increase in the number of scholars who are using historical data to examine contemporary theories of congressional politics across time. At the same time, an increasing number of political scientists are recognizing the importance of using the lessons of history to build more dynamic and generalizable theories of political phenemona. By collecting and using data encompassing a longer time horizon, we can be more confident that we are accounting for periods of both continuity and change in the areas of specific interest. Additionally, with a larger sample upon which to draw conclusions, we should be able to build more robust theories that explain a greater degree of observed variation in our political environment. Ultimately, the goal of this book is to increase our understanding of congressional elections across time by focusing on the unique electoral, institutional, and political changes that occurred in the late nineteenth and early twentieth centuries.

1.3 Plan of the Book

The organization of the book is as follows. In Chapter 2, we offer an overview of the academic literature and conventional wisdom about congressional elections prior to World War II. In particular, we describe how most accounts emphasize that elections held during the early part of this era were largely shaped by who was at the top of the ticket, leaving little room for candidate-specific factors or traits to influence election outcomes. At the same time, many who have written about this era would agree that the way candidates were chosen in the nineteenth and early twentieth centuries was bad for democracy and competition overall. Most accounts emphasize the fraud and corruption present across this period and reiterate that voters behaved as automatons, responding almost entirely to the interests of the party organizations who wielded nearly absolute control over the electoral machinery. We also discuss recent work by Alan Ware and John Reynolds that highlights the role of individual candidates in affecting elections during much of this era.

Chapter 3 describes the underlying theories that are examined more systematically in the subsequent chapters of the text. We begin by considering the ballot as a collective good and discussing how electoral reforms transformed the electoral environment from a party-run cartel to a political marketplace. This allows us to evaluate candidate and party behavior and demonstrate how party organizations of the late nineteenth and early twentieth centuries may have benefited from recruiting strong candidates for the ticket to enhance overall levels of electoral competitiveness. We elaborate upon the Strategic Politicians Theory developed by Jacobson and Kernell (1983) and examine how it might be equally applicable in a different era before the emergence of candidate-centered elections. In this chapter, we also discuss competing theoretical perspectives on the incumbency advantage in Congress and note how there are still a number of unanswered questions about the level of incumbent success over time. We argue that looking to the past can offer us new insights and valuable leverage with respect to this question given the significant differences in elections across various eras.

In the second part of Chapter 3, we point to a variety of questions that have yet to be addressed adequately in the congressional elections literature. For instance, what effect, if any, did candidate quality have on elections during this period? When, and under what conditions, did parties recruit strong candidates to run in the pre–Australian ballot era? What specifically can this tell us about the relationship between collective and individual responsibility in congressional elections? What factors contributed to the increased competitiveness of election campaigns during the late nineteenth century and why did this trend gradually decline over time? Is there evidence of an incumbency advantage during this era and, if so, where does it come from? As we discuss in the ensuing chapters, we believe answering these questions will offer new insights into this era, especially on how we view congressional elections compared with those held today. More importantly,

the second half of Chapter 3 sets up the discussion in the remainder
of the book to demonstrate how institutional change interacts with
the decisions of individual candidates and parties to further our understanding of electoral behavior and outcomes in congressional races
from this era.

Chapter 4 offers some initial comparisons between congressional
elections during the modern era and those from the past to better
illustrate instances of strategic behavior. We focus specifically on
trends highlighting the decline in competition over time in House races
and the growing incumbency advantage in elections. Along the way, we
discuss the archival research and data collection that were necessary to
undertake the analysis in the remainder of the book. Specifically, we
identify the main sources of electoral data (e.g., previous and current
two-party vote margins for candidates, party affiliation, presidential
vote in the congressional district) utilized in subsequent chapters in our
systematic analyses. We discuss the various procedures and sources
that were used to track down background data on candidates running in
House races from 1872–1944 and how we dealt with missing cases in our
data set. We also note the frequency and extent of partisan redistricting
in the late nineteenth and early twentieth centuries to allow us to assess
the impact this practice may have had on electoral competitiveness and
the incumbency advantage during this era. Furthermore, we consider
the various dates that states adopted the Australian ballot and direct
primary reforms. Using these data, we present preliminary trends that
begin to illuminate various electoral patterns such as the frequency of
experienced candidates running for office over time, the proportion of
districts with split outcomes between presidential and congressional
races, and the reelection rates of incumbent legislators.

Chapter 5 offers a central test of our theoretical expectations regarding the role of strategic politicians during this era. In particular, we
examine trends in strategic behavior among candidates for the House
from 1872–1944 in an attempt to better understand the impact of
electoral and institutional changes during this era. We evaluate several
changing patterns such as the emerging careerism in Congress, the
adoption of the Australian ballot, the introduction of the direct primary,
and the decline of strong party organizations during the twentieth century. We examine trends across the two parties to show how differences
may arise separately for Democrats and Republicans. We also consider
the effects of economic changes on elections during this period and
demonstrate that candidates made strategic entrance decisions based

on a variety of different electoral, institutional, and political factors including changing economic conditions at the state/national level. Additionally, we demonstrate how differences in ballot structure adopted in the early part of the twentieth century had notable implications for legislative behavior with respect to varying degrees of party unity among incumbents seeking reelection.

Chapter 6 focuses explicitly on the incumbency advantage and the decline in competition in congressional elections over time. We begin by briefly summarizing the voluminous literature on the incumbency advantage, noting that most of it has focused exclusively on the post–World War II era. We then argue that, by looking to the past, we can gain a comparative advantage on this puzzle which has perplexed scholars for nearly 40 years. As noted in subsequent chapters, we believe that the absence of many of the contemporary features of the U.S. Congress during this era will offer us leverage on both the sources and development of the incumbency advantage across time. We also examine strategic behavior on the part of both challengers and incumbents in an effort to demonstrate that the incumbency advantage that we identify is not simply an artifact of strategic exits in the form of retirements among incumbent legislators. Drawing upon recent literature on the incumbency advantage and applying it to this historical context, we show that candidate quality is an important and missing piece of the puzzle in explaining the incumbency advantage and the declining competition in congressional races. Additionally, we demonstrate that elections were more volatile during the nineteenth century due to the "insurance" system offered by the party organizations, which facilitated a greater number of quality challengers than we regularly observe during the modern era.

In the concluding chapter, we argue that collecting historical data and looking to the past has tremendous benefits for scholars who are interested in building and testing more dynamic theories of politics. In this context, we reiterate how gathering elections data for the U.S. House of Representatives from the late nineteenth and early twentieth centuries has assisted us in illuminating a variety of puzzles that have not been systematically addressed to date. We also briefly touch upon the normative implications of our findings in this chapter. In particular, we note that the "smoke-filled" nominating caucuses of the late nineteenth century may have been dens of coercion, fraud, and corruption in the electoral process, but the strong party organizations in control of this process were able to manufacture significantly higher levels of com-

petition in congressional races than we regularly observe today. With
the adoption of progressive reforms—such as the Australian ballot and
direct primary legislation at the turn of the century—such influence began to disappear as the parties were no longer able to entice otherwise
risk-averse candidates to seek elected office. Indeed, one of the direct
implications of our findings is that there could be a lot more potentially
winnable seats in the modern era if the party organizations could only
entice more experienced or quality candidates to run for office. As
long as strong candidates shy away from elective office, however, it is
difficult to imagine greater levels of electoral competitiveness becoming
the norm once again, especially if such reform comes with the risk of
corruption at the hands of revitalized party organizations.

2

History of U.S. House Elections

During the past five decades, much has been written about congressional elections in the post–World War II era, and the general patterns of election outcomes are clear and well-known by scholars. For instance, contemporary House elections produce relatively little turnover from one election cycle to the next and a dearth of competitive races in any given year. Even in more volatile recent elections such as 1994, 2006, and 2010 when control of the House chamber reverted to the other party, upwards of 90 percent of incumbents retained their seats. Incumbents are thought to accrue a number of advantages over rival candidates stemming from among other things, greater name recognition, enhanced fund-raising abilities, their record of legislative accomplishments, and a lack of strong opposition.

As the costs of contemporary congressional campaigns have continued to escalate in recent years, otherwise strong challengers have become more selective about entering races against incumbent candidates, as running and losing could put an end to a promising electoral career (Cox and Katz 2002; Jacobson 1989; Rohde 1979). State legislators, for instance, are often reluctant to run for a House seat since they typically have to give up their current position to wage what most likely will end up being an unsuccessful congressional campaign. With a limited number of strong candidates emerging to challenge sitting legislators except under the most ideal of conditions, incumbents have a much easier time getting reelected, which further enhances the view of members of Congress as entrenched politicians. As demonstrated by students of congressional elections, the risks and potential rewards of waging a competitive elective campaign have increased dramatically during the past 50 years.[1]

Despite the voluminous literature devoted to congressional elections in the post–World War II era, we think there are weaknesses in the literature on historical elections. The lack of a longitudinal perspective of elections means the literature has suffered from an inability to employ the institutional leverage that history offers to comment on a variety of empirical puzzles that cannot be addressed with contemporary data alone. The lack of systematic analyses of district-level results and candidate emergence patterns has led to an over reliance on anecdotal stories of mindless voting for party tickets, corruption, fraud, and other shady practices. Certainly, to some extent, these practices occurred, but we do think the prevalence of these things has been greatly overstated by authors who were advocates of Progressive era reforms, not dispassionate observers. To be sure, we are not the first to note this. In the pages that follow, we lay out the conventional story regarding elections in this era, note the recent contributions of historians and political scientists who have questioned this prevailing view, and set the stage for the theoretical and empirical arguments that fill the remaining pages of this volume.

2.1 The Era of Party Dominance

Without a doubt the most striking difference between congressional elections in the nineteenth century and those from the more modern era is the role that political parties played in structuring the ballot, both in terms of the form of the ballot and the names listed under each party banner. More generally, the institutional mechanisms in place during much of the nineteenth century also made it significantly easier for party organizations to exert control over candidate selection and the electoral process in general. For instance, parties were responsible for recruiting candidates and in designing the ballots voters would use to choose candidates. After several decades of near exclusive partisan control over the electoral machinery, this system was eventually supplanted by the adoption of the the Australian ballot in the 1890s and the direct primary in the early part of the twentieth century.

2.1.1 Candidate Recruitment

Candidate selection practices in the late nineteenth century were starkly different than they are today. In contrast to the familiar candidate-centered era of politics widespread today, elections during this era were largely party-centered (Jacobson 1989). Prior to the appearance of the direct primary in the early-to-mid part of the twentieth century, House candidates were chosen almost exclusively by party caucuses (Dallinger 1897; Ostrogorski 1964; Ware 2002). However, Ware (2002) notes that a few states employed party conventions to select candidates to run for local and statewide offices throughout the nineteenth century, but that the party organizations still exercised considerable control over the selection of individual candidates at these conventions. Their success in keeping unwanted challengers off the ballot stemmed largely from their organizational efforts, which allowed them to set the agenda at the conventions to their benefit.

The typical party caucus was dominated by coalitions of state and local party machines—themselves often comprised of smaller factional associations. These caucuses sought to nominate candidates that were loyal to the party, able to mobilize party followers, and, in doing so, enhance the overall attractiveness of the party ticket (Bensel 2004; Swenson 1982). The end result was a House chamber full of members who were beholden to the party machine. Since these members owed their seats to local party officials, they displayed a much greater degree of party loyalty. Additionally, and as Swenson (1982) notes, this effect became even more pronounced as careerism began to take hold during the late nineteenth century.

Incumbent House members who were interested in a career within the party had to continually display loyalty to the party if they wanted to regain the nomination in the subsequent election. Their career paths were much different as well. As Brady, Buckley, and Rivers (1999b) note, for much of the nineteenth century, legislators viewed their career as being within the political party and not necessarily in any individual office. Following the practice of "rotation" in office, which was utilized by the parties during the early part of this era, members of the House would often serve one or two terms before exiting the chamber (Kernell 1977; Silbey 1991; Struble 1979) and moving on to another political office. Some of this rotation was due to the fact that a seat in the U.S. House was not as prestigious as it is today due to the difficulties of travel, the relatively low salary for members serving in Congress, and the limited role of the federal government. In other cases, regular rotation was practiced to appease the various geographical units—often counties—within each congressional district.

Even as legislators gradually began to more consistently seek reelection over time, turnover in the House did not regularly fall below 50 percent until well into the 1880s (Fiorina, Rohde, and Wissel 1975; Kernell 1977). Although the late nineteenth century was clearly one of emerging careerism in the House, incumbents found that the lingering effects of rotation in office (Kernell 1977), highly competitive elections (Brady and Grofman 1991), and frequent congressional redistricting (Engstrom and Kernell 2005) all served as barriers to long congressional careers. Indeed, it was not until the early part of the twentieth century that the mean length of service for incumbent House members exceeded three terms (Polsby 1968).

2.1.2 Electoral Institutions

In addition to exercising tremendous control over the candidate selection process during this era, parties also yielded a considerable amount of influence over the voters through the balloting process. As Alan Ware (2002) maintains, the mid-nineteenth century witnessed a transformation from *viva voce* voting to voting via a party ballot. Under this system, party ballots were available at the polling place or handed out to voters in advance of the election. Parties typically employed different colored paper for their ballots to ensure that illiterate voters were using the proper ballot and to monitor the behavior of voters to ensure that they were voting for the "correct" candidates. This sentiment is echoed by Rusk (1970) who notes that prior to the adoption of the Australian ballot, voting was anything but a secret act as the distinctiveness of each party's ballot made it relatively easy for voters and poll watchers to identify which party's ballot was chosen and discourage voters from defecting from the party slate when they went to the polls.

The pseudomonopoly over access to the ticket enhanced the importance of party organizations during much of the nineteenth century. The use of the party ballot made it incredibly difficult for voters to split their tickets between candidates of different parties. For a voter to cast a split ticket, he would have to physically mark out or paste over one name on a party ballot and replace it with the candidate of his choice (Summers 2004). In an effort to discourage split-ticket voting, Summers (2004, 25) claims that party bosses would occasionally put oily substances on ballots to prevent voters from placing "pasters" over some of the names on the ballot or write in alternative candidate names since the oil would repel pencil marks. The act of splitting a ticket was cumbersome and was further discouraged because voting took place in full view of party workers who could easily monitor voters dropping their color-coded ticket into the ballot box (Bensel 2004; Engstrom and Kernell 2005; Rusk 1970).

Despite these potential constraints on the electorate, there is considerable evidence to suggest that some voters undertook such an act. Paul Kleppner (1983) estimates that roughly 10–12 percent of voters in the Western states cast split ballots for president and Congress during the latter part of the nineteenth century, with approximately 2 percent of voters in the North doing the same. Similarly, Reynolds and McCormick (1986) analyzed voting patterns in parts of New Jersey after 1880 and found that typically between 4 and 9 percent of voters failed to support the entire partisan ticket. For New York during this same period, they discovered that the incidence of split-ticket voting was significantly greater—upwards of 25 percent in certain parts of the state. The party ballot certainly made it more difficult for a voter to cast a ballot against a particular candidate of his party without defecting from the party altogether, but the preceding evidence suggests that voting a straight party ticket was certainly not universal in this era. Moreover, the absence of presidential candidates at the top of the ticket during midterm elections made it substantially more difficult to maintain partisan stability during these off-year elections. The presence of strong, national tides during the midterm would occasionally offset many of the gains made by the parties in the previous election, especially in years such as 1874, 1894 and 1938.

Beyond framing the choices offered to voters at the polls, parties also frequently altered congressional district boundaries to achieve more favorable partisan outcomes. To this point, Engstrom (2006) finds that political parties during this era regularly redrew district lines within states. State party officials were, thus, able to exploit changing political conditions to manipulate election outcomes at the state and ultimately national level. Despite the obvious lack of sophisticated GIS or mapping technology during the late nineteenth century, Engstrom (2006) demonstrates that parties maintained detailed voter registration records allowing them to manipulate the partisan balance in congressional districts fairly precisely at the time. Moreover, states exercised considerably more leeway during this era over when they would redraw district boundaries. District boundaries were redrawn as often or as infrequently as necessary to maximize the advantages accruing to the party in power.

Our own prior work with Engstrom (Carson, Engstrom, and Roberts

2006) found that regular redistricting combined with party control over the nomination of candidates served to significantly enhance the electoral prowess of the political party in power at the state level. When a congressional district was redrawn to the benefit of one political party, that party was more likely to recruit an experienced candidate to run in that race. This allowed parties to draw the electoral map in such a way that they could virtually assure themselves of narrow victories in an overwhelming majority of seats. On occasion, Engstrom (2006) notes that frequent partisan redistricting during the late nineteenth century meant the difference between winning a few additional seats and being in the majority (or minority), with all the procedural advantages that go along with such status.

2.2 Electoral Fraud

The strong party organizations of the nineteenth century, with their influence over numerous aspects of electoral politics, were able to manufacture heightened electoral competition in many parts of the country (Engstrom and Kernell 2005). Yet, this heightened competition came with considerable cost to democracy. The "smoke-filled" nominating caucuses of the nineteenth century were occasionally corrupt, always closed to the mass public, and part and parcel of an electoral system that provided incentives for party leaders to frequently employ coercive and fraudulent methods to win elections. While we may never fully know the extent to which party bosses and political machines manipulated election outcomes behind the scenes, there are numerous accounts of fraud and corruption that occurred at the voting booth. For example, Summers (2004, 110–112) offers a particularly disturbing account of electoral fraud during the latter half of the nineteenth century:

> [F]raud happened constantly and in a great enough amount to throw some elections into doubt...There were many ways of swelling a majority, especially in an era when states held their elections on different days. "Colonizations" would import voters from across state lines, lodge them in spare bedrooms over the saloons or in the flophouse district of major cities, hand them a list of the names under which they would claim to be registered, march them to the polls, pay them off, and send them home...Other voters gave home addresses that turned out to be lumberyards, vacant lots,

> and bonded warehouses...'Resurrectionists' complemented
> the colonizationist's skills. In every city, registered voters
> died or moved away between elections. But there was
> nothing like a close election for raising the dead. Well
> armed with appropriate names, impostors crowded the
> polls and voted as they had been paid to. A resourceful
> "resurrectionist" might vote again under a second name in
> the precinct next door.

In a similar vein, Richard Bensel (2004) offers an equally unsettling account of voting practices during the nineteenth century. Some voters during this era were willing to trade their votes for a shot of whiskey, a pair of boots, or sometimes even a few dollars. In describing the role of parties in this process, Bensel (2004, 3) explains that "Party agents seized on any device or tactic that might strengthen their ticket at the polls. When dealing with the lumpen proletariat of American democracy, these devices and tactics often included deception, petty bribery, and symbolic manipulation." At times, men were physically intimidated and prevented from voting at the polls by gangs or other representatives of the party machines. More common, however, was the practice of encouraging voters to avail themselves of one of the more common adages of the day: "vote early and vote often." In this respect, (Bensel 2004, 156–157) explains that the anonymity granted by the populations of large cities offered party machines the opportunity to entice voters to engage in fraud. Tactics included encouraging voters to vote in the same precinct more than once or in multiple precincts. Bensel also notes that parties occasionally intimidated election judges into accepting obviously fraudulent votes.

Many of the Progressive historians who have written about politics during this age emphasized these fraudulent accounts in order to delegitimize the election outcomes. They pointed out that the political parties wielded almost absolute control over access to the ballot, and claim that this resulted in carefully orchestrated victories and narrow defeats alongside the massive amounts of corruption and fraud in the electoral process. In writing about the role of political machines in the late nineteenth century, for instance, Josephson (1938, 92–94), paints a hyperbolic portrait of the influence of party bosses in the political process:

> The boss was the nearly absolute ruler of his State Or-
> ganization; but in turn he was compelled, as regularly as

the medieval lord of the manor, to nourish and protect his vassals and all his manor hands. For without their disciplined labor the substance of his power would vanish. The Senator-boss was in a sense enslaved to his ever hungry Organization; its quenchless appetite, like that of a legendary dragon, calling for ever more nutriment, more spoils, made for him "white nights" of torment over the problems of discovering patronage and favor enough to meet the demands of his followers, and days of unwearied search for all offices which be turned to his army.

Other historians writing about electoral politics during the late nineteenth century suggest that the way candidates were chosen prior to the adoption of the direct primary was detrimental for competition and democracy overall. Consider the following account by Robert Cherny, who describes electoral politics in the United States during the Gilded Age:

During much of the nineteenth century, the process of choosing a party's candidates for office and determining its stance on current issues theoretically began among the party's voters...Voters who attended the primaries chose their party's candidates for any elective offices in their township, ward, or precinct...Theoretically, then, any voter could participate in this exercise in grass-roots democracy. However, widespread participation in the primaries was not typical, especially in urban areas, partly because few issues or candidates motivated a significant turnout, but mainly because members of the local party organization often found it advantageous to discourage a large attendance. (Cherny 1997, 6)

In the end, increased electoral competition may have been a byproduct of the existing practices and electoral rules in place, but corruption, fraud, and voter intimidation became an unwanted and undesirable consequence as well. Over time, popular discontent with these activities became widespread enough that the electoral system itself was subject to widespread and growing criticism by the end of the nineteenth century.

2.3 Progressive Era Reforms

Dissatisfaction with electoral practices was not limited to the Progressive reformers as party organizations gradually began to identify the need for changes to the existing system as well. In an era of highly competitive elections with relatively close electoral margins, the parties recognized the need for greater order and stability within the electoral system. As early as the 1880s, and despite the highly partisan nature of the electorate, coordination problems began to plague even the most well-oiled party machines across the country. This was especially true with respect to regulating the behavior of local party actors who began to more regularly disagree with the agenda of the state and national parties. In discussing the specific nature of the problems with balloting during this era, Ware (2002, 36–37) notes that the party ballot led to a series of party management and coordination problems. In particular, weak party identification among voters led to widespread ticket splitting by the early 1880s. Party decentralization meant that county party organizations could more easily deviate from the electoral strategies of state and national parties. At the same time, "party freelancers" would often distribute ballots that mimicked the official party ballots, albeit with one or more names changed or replaced. Taken as a whole, the portrait of the party organizations in full control of the ballot distribution process was often a mirage.

One of the major constraints that parties faced during this era is that they had to supply ballots to voters who would be voting on a wide range of elective offices across the county and state. To ensure that all of the local races were included on the regional ballots, parties would turn over the responsibility for creating the ballots to county and local party organizations. Alan Ware describes how factionalism within county parties sometimes yielded "bolters" who would select their own candidates for certain offices, but would act as though they were allied with the candidates higher up on the party ticket. The problem arose from the lack of centralization within the party organizations and only grew worse over time. While the county or state party organization might favor a specific candidate for a particular office, they were often at the mercy of the local parties who did not always respond to the same norms, ideals, and incentives. This stemmed largely from the unofficial nature of the nomination process at the local level, which lacked strict rules and procedures, further contributing to coordination problems for the party organization. In particular, Ware (2002, 37) notes that:

> It was not even necessary for "bolters" to have the resources
> to produce a complete ballot of their own—many did not.
> Without their vote becoming invalid, voters were permitted
> to strike out the names of candidates on the ballot for
> whom they did not wish to vote, and they could substitute
> the names of alternative persons for whom they did wish
> to vote—by sticking on what was called a "paster" to the
> relevant part of the ballot. The supporters of "bolters"
> would supply the appropriate "pasters" to voters before
> they got to the polling place.

This type of malfeasance was becoming more widespread by the late
1880s, which further compounded the problems faced by the county
and state party organizations in their attempt to manipulate outcomes
at the district level (Reynolds and McCormick 1986). Eventually, the
coordination problems reached crisis proportions as the population
continued to grow and the party organizations lost their grip over
county and local parties.

The magnitude of control that the party organizations had previously wielded over the electoral process rapidly began to unravel
around the turn of the century because of these and other problems.
At the same time, party machines began to lose a certain degree of
influence over electoral outcomes due to the progressive reform movement that led to the widespread adoption of the Australian or secret
ballot. It is clear that electoral accountability was greatly enhanced
in the 1890s by the rapid adoption of the Australian ballot across
the states (Albright 1942; Evans 1917; Kernell 1977; Rusk 1970). In
essence, this institutional change made it easier for voters to reward
or punish elected officials individually since all candidates for elected
offices would now be listed on the same ballot. The Australian ballot
also provided incumbents with the institutional means to develop a
"personal vote" with their constituents as they could now be rewarded
or punished selectively based on their level of responsiveness to the
voters (Cain, Ferejohn, and Fiorina 1992; Katz and Sala 1996).[2] Moreover, Engstrom and Kernell (2005) emphasize that "the secret ballot
removed voters from the steady gaze of party workers, and second, the
new state-supplied ballots made it easier for voters to cross party lines
in selecting candidates for different offices."

Somewhat surprisingly, recent evidence suggests that the major party organizations were not initially opposed to the idea of the secret ballot and, in many cases, actually supported its eventual adoption within the states. In particular, Alan Ware (2002) argues that parties viewed the adoption of the Australian ballot as a mechanism for dealing with the increased agency loss stemming from the delegation of power to wards and local party chairs. The uniform ballot prepared by the states provided reduced opportunities for local officials to sabotage the party ballot, which had been occurring with increasing regularity unless the local party organizations were offered concessions by the state parties. Moreover, state party machines found it difficult to manage political affairs at the local level as a greater number of voters began to reside in urban areas. With the evolution from a rural, agrarian society to a more urbanized one, party workers lost touch with voters and had a much more difficult time getting party ballots into the hands of voters since it became more difficult to identify who was eligible to vote in growing urban areas. Finally, the economic incentives became too strong for the parties to resist the change to adopt a uniform ballot. Shifting responsibility for the considerable costs from the parties to the state government for generating ballots meant that the costs of preparing the ballots would be transferred as well. This freed up considerable revenue that could be put to better uses by the party organizations.

For many of the same reasons, Ware (2002) argues that parties at the turn of the century did not initially view the adoption of the direct primary as a threat to their political power. Although the use of direct primaries did not catch on as quickly as the Australian ballot, it was actually the success associated with the secret ballot that convinced the major party organizations of the day that this method of candidate selection would be largely compatible with their partisan interests. Indeed, once the first "modern" direct primary was adopted in Minnesota in 1899, reform of the nomination system spread quickly across the country during the next 15 years. Thus, while it may seem as though the major parties were forced to surrender a considerable amount of their power at the hands of "anti-party" reformers, Ware (2002) maintains that the parties were actually willing accomplices in the rapid and successful adoption of this reform effort. This was true, in part, because potential office seekers were more aggressive in lobbying party officials for nominations.

Furthermore, and according to Reynolds (2006, 62–104), candidates began to more aggressively court nominations openly and actively from party conventional delegates, a practice that was unheard of prior to this time. These "hustling" candidates had the effect of lessening the party's ability to select candidates given that these outwardly ambitious candidates now controlled campaign resources and presumably votes. Party insiders were still formally participating in nominating conventions, yet they found that their choices were effectively limited by the strategies of this new style of candidate. One result of this development was a weakening of the party's resolve against primary reform, which seemed to be growing more inevitable as the years passed.

Both Alan Ware and John Reynolds agree that the major parties and the string of politicians who would be elected under this new selection mechanism failed to anticipate the long-term consequences of such reform and its effects on their own power base. As Ware notes:

> Constrained as they were by public attitudes to parties, and engaging in a public debate that increasingly was about direct nominations, elected politicians, therefore, came increasingly to disregard the fact that the impact of such nominations on party interests was largely unknown and that they could have adverse consequences for the nomination process. Caution was abandoned in favor of a "quick fix." The result was the enactment of a reform that, in the long term was to contribute to the transformation of America's parties in ways that those who passed such legislation could not have foreseen, and would not have endorsed. (Ware 2002, 224)

As a result of these major institutional reforms, elected representatives found that their individual incentives had substantially changed. Whereas the candidates had previously been beholden to party officials, they now found themselves reporting directly to the voters. This is where individual responsibility begins to supplant collective responsibility and representatives begin to pursue actions that individually foster their own reelection. With the widespread adoption of the Australian ballot across the states, voters could more easily vote for one party's candidate for president while choosing the other party's candidate for representative, thus separating the fate of the individual candidate from that of his party. This trend would continue over the next several decades, further contributing to the style of representative behavior more familiar in the modern era.

Voters were also given greater input into the candidate selection process with the adoption and emergence of the direct primary in the early part of the twentieth century. These changes were extraordinary and had a profound effect on the party organizations that had previously monopolized the electoral process. Although the party organizations initially thought they could continue to influence candidate selection even after adoption of the direct primaries, it became clear over time that parties had less control over the "quality" of the candidates running for office (Ware 2002, 231). What is less clear is the long-term effect of these reforms on electoral competition.[3] During the late nineteenth century, it was not unusual for approximately half of all winning candidates to receive less than 55 percent of the vote in congressional races. However, by the 1920s, less than 20 percent of congressional elections were decided by such a narrow margin, suggesting a substantial decline in electoral competitiveness. Whether or not the two factors are related remains as yet unclear.

Initially, the party organizations tried to maintain some semblance of control over candidates following the widespread adoption of the Australian ballot by regulating the *type* of ballot that was in use. The parties specifically favored adoption of the party column ballot as opposed to the office bloc ballot since the latter focused more attention on the "individual" qualities of the candidates rather than the party labels. In states that adopted the office bloc ballot, for instance, the parties pressed hard to include a box that could be checked off by the voters who wanted to vote a straight ticket at the polls, thus negating the effects of candidate quality initially (Ware 2002). As more states began to adopt some form of the office bloc ballot during the twentieth century, however, this began weakening the coattail effect in presidential elections and made it substantially easier for incumbents to begin cultivating a "personal vote" with their constituents. With the gradual adoption of the direct primary in the early twentieth century, the major parties found it cumbersome to coordinate entry decisions of individual candidates, which made it increasingly difficult for them to win campaigns as a team as they once did. With each passing election in the early twentieth century, parties were losing their grip over the electoral system they had once firmly controlled.

2.4 The Way Forward

The brief survey of the literature on historical elections sets the stage for the theoretical and data analysis that follows. After sifting through archival sources, election results, newspaper stories, and various other historical documents, we have come to the conclusion that voters from this era were attentive, informed, and quite active in politics. Contrary to the perception of voting behavior that is often depicted by historians, voters from this era were not automatons blindly following the will of the party machines. They were active in learning about candidates and the parties and voted in large numbers. Ironically, this is largely consistent with how voters were portrayed during the early part of the nineteenth century, but various historical accounts seem to suggest that they somehow lost their way after the party organizations became more powerful in the postbellum era.

Additionally, our investigation of congressional elections during this era strongly suggests that candidates for elective office have always been ambitious and have sought to gain office through the most direct mechanism possible. During the late nineteenth century, this meant gaining the nomination and support of the local party machines—either through conventional means or by campaigning for it (Reynolds 2006). At the same time, party organizations benefited from having strong, experienced candidates on the ballot since their ultimate goal was to maximize their number of seats in Congress. Indeed, for a time, elections during this era were highly competitive as a result of a large number of experienced or quality candidates facing off against one another. With the adoption of a number of Progressive era reforms, however, the influence of party machines gradually began to fade, which accelerated the shift from party-centered to more candidate-centered elections over time.

The analysis in the remainder of the book largely supports the arguments of scholars such as Kleppner (1983), Ware (2002), and Reynolds (2006), while casting doubt on the anecdotal accounts of Progressive historians. More specifically, we test many of their arguments about the effects of Australian ballot reform, the adoption of the direct primary, and declining party influence on candidate competition in House races during the late nineteenth and early twentieth centuries. By doing so, we uncover new insights about congressional elections from this era that help us understand how elections have both evolved over time and become substantially less competitive.

3

Institutional Change and Candidate Behavior

3.1 Congressional Candidates in a Partisan Era

Congressional elections were very different affairs in the late nineteenth century than they would be in the early 1900s or in the years immediately preceding World War II. The late nineteenth century was the pinnacle of partisan control of congressional elections (Brady, Buckley, and Rivers 1999a). Party machines exercised enormous control over nearly every aspect of the nomination and ballot process from the selection of candidates to stand for each office to the printing and distribution of the ballots that voters used to choose candidates. Party control over the machinery of elections loosened considerably with the adoption of the direct primary and various forms of the Australian ballot in the early decades of the twentieth century. However, the congressional elections literature suggests that a strong candidate-centered system did not emerge in the United States until after the conclusion of World War II. Our argument in this chapter, and more broadly throughout the book, is that many of the important dynamics of congressional elections across time remain unexplored. For example, how did the weakening party control over the machinery of elections affect the behavior of strategic politicians and election outcomes. Did the adoption of the direct primary affect the dynamics of challenger emergence in congressional races? More broadly, how did the changes in electoral institutions affect electoral competition in the United States? This chapter builds the theoretical foundation that we use to provide the evidence for how electoral institutions shaped the behavior of candidates, parties, and voters from 1872–1944.

Due to the almost complete control by parties over the machinery of elections during this era, one would imagine that it would have been difficult—if not impossible—for incumbents or other candidates to develop anything akin to a "personal vote" (Cain, Ferejohn, and Fiorina 1987) since citizens were voting for a party slate and could not easily make office-by-office choices. Swenson (1982, 20) argues that party machines purposefully recruited "docile" candidates rather than those with large personal followings. His account suggests that candidates were selected not for their vote getting abilities, but rather for their loyalty to the party organization. Unlike today's congressional elections, decisions about whether to seek a place on the ballot were typically not left up to the individual candidates. As Ostrogorski (1964, 196) notes, "Being aware of the fact that the [party] machine holds the keys of the electoral situation ... The candidates of the party are the first to realize that they are not at liberty to attain their object independently of the Machine and still less in opposition to it."

Few would argue that consistently putting party above the interests of constituents is a useful strategy if one is trying to cultivate a long-term relationship with one's constituency. However, parties from this era were more concerned with maintaining the collective reputation of the party than with recruiting candidates with large personal followings. As Swenson (1982) notes, scholars who have written about this era point out that the electoral institutions in place allowed parties to pursue their collective interests while retarding the individual candidates to leverage their personal reputation. Given these institutional arrangements, it is not surprising that the late nineteenth century is characterized as one of the most polarized as reflected by high degrees of party unity in congressional voting (Poole and Rosenthal 1997).

These arguments are certainly not without merit; nevertheless, our own prior research on this subject suggests that this account is far too simplistic and does not adequately explain variation in observed outcomes. We have demonstrated, for instance, that party organizations often sought to recruit experienced candidates to run in competitive congressional districts. Indeed, Carson and Roberts (2005) find that candidates with prior electoral experience were more likely to be nominated for office when national and local conditions favored their candidacy. National economic conditions, an incumbent with a small prior margin of victory, and the absence of an incumbent in a particular district were all directly related to experienced candidates' entry decisions. Similarly, we have shown that incumbents and experienced candidates during this era responded to changes in district boundaries brought on by congressional redistricting. Incumbents and strategic politicians ran when House districts were drawn favorably and bailed out when facing an adverse gerrymander (Carson et al. 2006).

Furthermore, Engstrom (2006) has clearly shown that parties in the late nineteenth century regularly manipulated district lines for short-term political gain. The electoral effects of these manipulations were enhanced by the nomination process. Competitive districts attracted experienced candidates from both parties while non-competitive districts saw imbalances in quality candidates on the parties' respective ballots. As *The New York Times* reported in the wake of the redistricting plan designed by Ohio Democrats in 1890:

> In some of the newly made districts there will be woe and heaviness of spirit between the time of nomination and election day. No one will more keenly realize this than [Republican] Hon. T.E. Burton of the Cleveland district. He is in a gerrymandered district where a Democratic majority is almost a certainty; *he is sure to be pitted against the strongest man the Democrats can name.* (italics added, *The New York Times*, July 25, 1890, p. 5, col. 5)

Recent work by John Reynolds (2006) bolsters our argument on this point. His thorough examination of nominating conventions in the late nineteenth and early twentieth centuries argues that "candidate-centered" politics is in no way a post–World War II phenomenon. In fact, his research demonstrates that political entrepreneurs often hijacked party nominating conventions and used their purported skills as vote getters to justify why they should receive the party nomination. These ambitious, hustling candidates

> ... entered the political arena through contests for more local offices. Here they learned to greet voters, make speeches, and even employ advertising on their own behalf. They put the electioneering skills they mastered in running for lesser offices to use as they sought higher positions. They worked hard at getting themselves or at least their names before the public. (Reynolds 2006, 80)

As we develop and elaborate more fully below, we believe that Reynolds is correct in arguing there was more driving nominations and

elections in the late nineteenth century than simple loyalty to the local
party organizations—the candidates themselves had a discernible effect
on election outcomes.

3.1.1 The Ballot as a Collective Good

Why would state or national party organizations have cared about the
vote getting abilities for down ticket offices in the party ballot era?
The short answer is that we believe that presidential candidates were
far from the only factor influencing the decisions of voters in the latter
half of the nineteenth century. As early as the 1850s, members of the
House were able to propose and secure passage of legislation that was
local in nature or what we would today refer to as "pork"(Baughman
2008; Finocchiaro and Rohde 2008). With elections looming every
two years, representatives recognized the tangible benefits of funneling
distributive benefits back to their districts as often as possible in an
attempt to increase their reelection prospects. Additionally, as Brady
et al. (1999a) note, congressional elections were hypercompetitive in
the late nineteenth century. Much like contemporary elections during
the past decade, each party entered the election season with a high
degree of uncertainty as to who would attain majority status in the
upcoming Congress. This uncertainty had the effect of increasing the
marginal value of each additional House seat that could be won.

Therefore, in addition to needing a strong get-out-the-vote operation
to make sure loyal partisans went to the polls on Election Day, parties
also needed "good" candidates to run for elective office. Consistent
with a well established literature on political parties, we view parties in
this era as teams united for the purpose of winning elections (Aldrich
1995; Brady et al. 1999a; Cox and McCubbins 1993). Accordingly, the
quality of the ballot is a collective good for each member of the party.
As such, across all offices, there are likely to be spillover effects as
many voters make essentially one choice—which party to support. A
strong congressional candidate can yield spillover votes both above and
below him on the ticket. The flip side of the relationship, of course, is
that a weak candidate for a particular office could severely damage the
fortunes of other candidates given the collective nature of the partisan
ballot.

Kolodny (1998) provides considerable evidence that fear of weak
presidential candidates was the primary force behind the creation
of congressional campaign committees in the mid-nineteenth century.

The party ballot—and to a lesser extent the party column form of the Australian ballot—organized the voters' choices by party, rather than simply a collection of individual choices on a ballot. As such, party organizations needed to be concerned about how the candidate for each office on the ballot would affect the collective reputation of the party with voters. Given the inherent difficulties associated with casting a split ticket, parties had to fear that a "bad" candidate or set of candidates could lead a voter to abstain, or worse, cast a ballot for an opposing party.

As Engstrom and Roberts (2009) note, ballot law changes in Maryland were motivated by the state Democratic leadership's wish to distance themselves from what they perceived to be weak and unpopular presidential campaigns of William Jennings Bryan in the 1890s. Clearly, parties had to be concerned about the individual effect that each candidate would have on the parties' reputation with potential voters. As such, they attempted to recruit the strongest possible candidates to run in House races that they thought were potentially competitive. After all, the more vote getting ability each individual candidate contributes to the collective good (the ballot), the greater the party's collective output (votes and offices) (Alchian and Demsetz 1972). Further, before the adoption of the direct primary in the early twentieth century, parties had many tools at their disposal to help control who ultimately received the party nomination. This control allowed the parties to insure they had the optimal collection of candidates across the ballot.

Throughout our analysis we distinguish between "quality" candidates (i.e. those who have previously held elective office) and non-quality candidates (i.e. those who have never held elective office of any type). This is admittedly a blunt instrument for measuring candidate quality, but one that has proven to be quite adept at capturing vote getting ability both in the contemporary era (Jacobson 1989) and in the late nineteenth century (Carson and Roberts 2005). Indeed, this simple dichotomous measure consistently outperforms more nuanced measures of quality that seek to differentiate between levels of office or types of background experience (Jacobson 1989). In addition, we are quite certain that more elaborate measures of candidate quality would be impossible to collect during much of the time period under analysis here.[1]

What kinds of "qualities" do we believe experienced candidates brought to the partisan ticket? The most important quality was the ability to marshal additional votes for the party ticket. Skilled, well-known candidates could enhance the attractiveness of the overall ticket for prospective voters. Given that presidential candidates rarely travelled during the early period we analyze, and lacked an extensive get-out-the-vote operation, campaign mobilization efforts typically proceeded in a bottom-up fashion. While presidential candidates often waged front-porch campaigns, it was left up to the candidates for state and local offices to stump for the ticket on the campaign trail. In an era of torchlight parades and door-to-door canvassing, skilled campaigners were critical for rallying the party faithful. Quite often the real danger to party fortunes was that loyal partisan supporters would abstain from voting (Summers 2004). Thus, voter turnout was critical and rousing orators could help mobilize partisans to win close elections. In 1876, for instance, *The New York Times* attributed overall Republican successes in Ohio and Indiana to the strong mobilization efforts of the Republican congressional candidates:

> It is worthy of note that the excellent character of Congressional nominations in Ohio and Indiana brought out the full strength of the party in a way that nothing else could have done. All the energetic canvass of the State tickets, with the aid of the national organization and many outside laborers, was not worth so much—valuable as it was—as the sterling character of the Congressional candidates in doubtful districts. (*The New York Times*, October 12, 1876, 4)

Although it was in the best interests of the parties to maximize the number of strong candidates running in all ballot slots, the self-interest of individual politicians could have run afoul of the collective goal of putting together a strong partisan ticket (or campaigning to help get out the vote). Even as local and state party machines attempted to maximize the aggregate number of quality candidates appearing on the ballot in a given year, the individual incentives of prospective candidates are to run only when they are likely to secure the office (Jacobson and Kernell 1983; Rohde 1979). Thus, when a party is likely to win a seat, an oversupply of candidates willing to pay the costs of emergence should be likely to emerge. Yet, in seats that are not "sure wins," there will be fewer quality candidates willing to bear the costs of campaigning and risk losing. Ironically, it is the seats with uncertain outcomes where having a quality candidate can yield the largest marginal effect on the election. This is where we argue that parties played a outsized role in increasing overall electoral competition in this era.

How did parties ensure that the collective good—in this case the quality of candidates on the ballot—was adequately supplied? We argue that the hierarchical, firm-like nature of party organizations along with their cartel-like control over the machinery of elections allowed parties to overcome the collective action problems and transaction costs inherent in ballot formation (Coase 1937). Late nineteenth century parties clearly had an incentive to coordinate entry decisions and compel reluctant candidates to run for office. Their solution to this problem, as Brady et al. (1999a) persuasively demonstrate, was to offer "insurance" to losing candidates. Candidates were guaranteed other positions of influence that the party controlled in exchange for their partisan loyalty. This insurance mechanism aided the parties in recruiting otherwise risk-averse candidates to run in competitive races since they recognized that losing did not necessitate a premature end to their political ambitions.

As Brady et al. (1999a) detail, for much of the nineteenth century, politicians viewed their career as being within the state party organization rather than in any particular elective office. It was not unusual for House members to serve a term or two, move to a different elective office, and then return to the U.S. House. The parties' cartel-like control over ballot access had vast effects on the entry and exit decisions of individual candidates. First, ambitious politicians discovered that the only viable way of attaining elective office was through a party nomination, which resulted in a strong incentive to join a party organization (Aldrich 1995). Second, in order to keep in good standing with the party, ambitious politicians needed to be flexible about when and where they would seek office in order to best serve the needs of the party organizations. Third, and most importantly, parties could mitigate the opportunity costs of running in a tough to win seat by offering losing candidates insurance. In congressional districts across the country, party leaders were able to carefully select candidates who would contribute to the collective good of the ticket. This led to a plentiful supply of quality candidates willing to enter races, since the potential costs of running and losing were largely underwritten by the party organization.[2]

To see this more clearly, consider equation 3.1 below in which we modify the standard candidate entry model to better reflect the calculus facing nineteenth century candidates:

$$E(r) = p(b) - c + Insurance \qquad (3.1)$$

The first part of the equation is the standard rational entry model where the expected utility of running for an office r is a function of the probability of victory p, the benefit of the target office b, and the monetary and opportunity costs of running c. The addition of the *Insurance* term represents the payment—in the form of a patronage position or a promise of future opportunities to run for office—the party is willing to offer a prospective candidate in the event that he loses an electoral contest in a specific election year. Given that the *Insurance* term is non-negative, the costs of entry will be directly subsidized by the party organization. With the subsidized costs of office seeking, we would expect to see a larger supply of quality candidates in seats that are marginally competitive at best, as the party provided subsidy for running effectively bids down the effective costs of entry for candidates. This situation was a "win-win" for both political parties and candidates as Brady et al. (1999a, 12) point out that "Candidates benefited ... because they were insured of a political career even if they lost an election ... [and] Parties benefited because ... they could recruit 'good' candidates to run for office."

When considering the calculus of candidate entry, it is reasonable to think that the costs of running and winning during this period were substantially lower than in the modern era of candidate-centered elections. As Jacobson (2009) explains, candidates today largely run political campaigns independent of party organizations. Although the contemporary parties can help with mobilizing voters and offering valuable support services to candidates, the candidates do much of the legwork themselves. During the late nineteenth and early twentieth centuries, however, the party organizations handled most of the electoral machinery themselves. They recruited candidates to run for elective office, distributed information to the electorate, covered most of the candidates' expenses associated with running a political campaign, and mobilized voters on election day. Candidates were responsible for informing the citizens about the party platform—especially during non-presidential years—but the costs that are typically paid for by candidates themselves in the modern era were largely subsidized by the party organizations in the postbellum era in exchange for the candidates' loyalty to the party organization.

While our account draws heavily from Brady et al. (1999a), our point of departure is with the direction of causality. They argue that a large number of competitive elections was a necessary condition for the formation of the parties' cartel-like control over the machinery of elections and the insurance system that kept it running efficiently. In contrast, we view competitive elections as a byproduct of strong party control of the electoral machinery, not a necessary condition for strong parties at the local level. As we develop throughout the remainder of the book, election reforms at the turn of the century fundamentally changed the calculus for both political parties and individual candidates, eventually leading to fewer quality candidates and an overall decline in competitiveness of U.S. House elections.

The combination of ballot reform and the direct primary ended the parties' firm-like control over ballot access and effectively created a "market" for candidate entry. With the demise of party control over the electoral machinery, the party subsidy on ballot entry was removed. This had the effect of bidding up the costs of emergence and resulted in a reduced supply of experienced candidates willing to take up their party's banner (Alford and Brady 1989). As such, we contend that the cartel-like nature of the electoral system, with strong party organizations controlling access to the ballot, helped ensure a better crop of congressional candidates running on the slate as opposed to the market-driven system that is more common in today's candidate-centered environment.

3.2 Australian Ballot Reform and Candidate Behavior

Within a relatively short period of time, states adopted both the Australian ballot and the direct primary as the means of nominating candidates for office. In this section, we briefly discuss the parties' motivations in acquiescing to the adoption of the Australian ballot, followed by a discussion of how the widespread adoption of the Australian ballot affected congressional elections. In particular, we present our theoretical expectations for how these institutional changes affected the behavior of strategic politicians over time.

3.2.1 Parties, Agency Loss, and the Australian Ballot

By the mid-1880s, the Australian or secret ballot was becoming common in Western European countries. The first legislation providing for the

Australian ballot in the United States was enacted by the Kentucky state legislature in 1888 and applied only to the city of Louisville. Later in 1888, Massachusetts became the first state to adopt a statewide Australian ballot (Ware 2002). Other states quickly followed and by the turn of the century, the Australian ballot was prevalent throughout the United States. Why was the parties' control over the ballot so easily dispensed with throughout the country? The answers are numerous, but a close reading of the historical record suggests that a move away from party printed ballots was favored by a coalition of anti-party "bolters," Mugwumps, Populists, and agrarian activists (Fredman 1968). Recent evidence also exists suggesting the major political parties were supporters of ballot reform as well for a variety of different reasons (Ware 2002).

The motives of the anti-party groups and "good government" re-formers in seeking ballot reform are relatively clear. The Mugwumps, in particular, were a faction of the Republican Party that initially split off in the 1884 presidential election as a result of the perceived corruption association with James Blaine, the Republican candidate for president. Their discontent continued for the next few elections and eventually manifested itself in terms of support for ballot reform due to perceptions of irregularities in the voting process and their lack of loyalty to the complete Republican ticket. For most reformers and party bolters, the status quo of allowing the party regulars to prepare and distribute ballots rendered it extremely difficult for minor parties and factions of larger parties to secure party nominations and elective office. The party bosses had no incentive, of course, to list the names of those candidates who were not certain to be loyal to the party agenda. Indeed, for a non–party favored candidate to win office, he/she would have either had to print and distribute their own ballot or convince a plurality of voters to "knife" a major party candidate's name on the party ballot and "paste" in the name of the outsider candidate (Reynolds 2006).

A state printed and controlled ballot also reduced the possibilities for electoral corruption. Corruption and coercion were not uncommon features of elections under the party ballot, as the combination of party controlled ballots and public casting of ballots opened the door for party workers to influence the votes of citizens (Bensel 2004; Summers 2004). Parties were free to print ballots of different sizes, colors, and even scents so as to make it easier for party workers and voters to identify the "correct" ballot. Stories of electoral fraud are widespread, colorful, and horrifying for those who believe strongly in democratic principles of governance. Nevertheless, Kleppner (1987) points out that the charges of electoral fraud were rarely substantiated and almost always exaggerated to include such behavior as "voting one's narrow self-interest."[3] Kleppner also maintains that the motives of the reformers were not as pure as they would have us believe as their overriding goal was to restrict the suffrage rights of poor, uneducated, and illiterate immigrants. In fact, these self-proclaimed "better citizens" did not think that these individuals were worthy of participating in the electoral process. Although many factors other than ballot reform can affect turnout, it is clear that after the widespread adoption of the Australian ballot, turnout fell from near 80 percent in 1896 to less than 60 percent by 1912 (Stonecash 2008).

Given the long-term effects of ballot reform, the more interesting question is why did the major parties not do more to stop reform efforts? Ware (2002) offers the best treatment of this subject, providing several reasons for parties to embrace reform efforts, the most compelling being that the party ballot did not offer the parties as much control over electoral outcomes as many believed. The gradual transformation of the U.S. population from largely rural to more urban made it increasingly difficulty for party workers and party voters to identify each other at the polls. This was especially problematic for party officials, as they could no longer be sure they were getting their ballots into the hands of the "proper" voters nor could they be sure voters were casting the "proper" ballot given the ease of producing similar looking ballots. Occasionally, local factions would use their control over the ballot to extort concessions from the state or national party organizations. If the local factions were not bought off they would engage in what Reynolds and McCormick (1986) labeled political "treachery." As Reynolds and McCormick (1986) claim, this malfeasance took various forms including not placing the proper candidates on the ballot, "knifing" through certain names on the ballot, and encouraging the use of "pasters" that allowed the name of a party nominee to be covered up with a different name altogether. One example they highlight documents a case in 1878 where the Chair of the Republican State Committee mailed "fifty sheets of pasters to party officials around the state," and suggested that "You will of course fully understand their use and will dispose of them as you deem necessary" (Reynolds and McCormick 1986, 127).

In short, the changing population demographics created large information asymmetries as state party bosses could not be sure if their local subordinates were printing and distributing the proper ballot. Without an effective monitoring system, party organizations suffered increased agency loss as they tried to corral their various local factions and voters. Parties briefly experimented with oil based ballots to prevent the use of "pasters," but that did not prevent other forms of treachery such as simply printing the "wrong" name on the ballot (Bensel 2004; Summers 2004). With their control over the electoral machinery diminishing, party organizations looked for effective solutions that would help them regain the advantage they once had in electoral politics.

For the major parties, the Australian ballot was appealing on a number of levels. With a state printed ballot, a party organization could be sure that its preferred candidates would appear on the ballot with its label affixed to the candidates' names. This effectively reduced the agency loss associated with the ballot to zero, as parties could be sure that the correct candidates' names were listed on the ballot. Besides helping to stabilize the electoral process for parties, Australian ballot reform also shifted the considerable cost of ballot printing from the party to the state and local governments, hence freeing up more party funds for the mobilization of voters. Consequently, Ware (2002) argues that parties quickly chose to try and control the *type* of Australian ballot adopted rather than standing in the way of reform. As we discuss more fully in Chapter 4, no fewer than five forms of the Australian ballot were adopted in the American states with several states changing the type of ballot regularly in response to evolving political conditions. The most basic distinction in ballot type was between the party column ballot (see Figure 3.1 for an example), which listed each party's candidates for individual offices in a column on the ballot, and the office bloc ballot (see Figure 3.2 for an example), which listed the candidates for each office on the ballot by office. The two major parties had a strong preference for the party column ballot, as it most closely approximated the form of the party ballot and was more likely to elicit the desired straight-ticket voting.

3.2.2 Candidates and the Australian Ballot

How did the switch from the party ballot to the Australian ballot affect the strategic behavior of candidates and, in turn, election outcomes? Rusk (1970), Kernell (1977), and Katz and Sala (1996) all contend that electoral accountability was greatly enhanced by adoption of the Australian ballot. Theoretically, this is sensible. The Australian ballot

Figure 3.1: Sample Party Column Ballot

SPECIAL INSTRUCTIONS

1. Make all of your selections BEFORE pushing the green VOTE button located below the lower right corner of the ballot.

2. Select your choice by pressing the "X" to the right of the person's name. Once you press the "X", you will see a red light at the upper left corner of that "X". This indicates your choice.

3. If you want to change your choice, press the "X" again and the light will go out. Then, press the "X" to the right of your choice to make a new selection.

4. Make sure that a red light is lit at the upper left corner of the "X" for ALL of your choices BEFORE pushing the green VOTE button to cast your ballot.

FOR		DEMOCRATIC PARTY	REPUBLICAN PARTY	GREEN PARTY	INDEPENDENT PARTY OF DELAWARE	LIBERTARIAN PARTY
UNITED STATES SENATOR VOTE FOR ONE (1)	Write In	THOMAS R. CARPER	JAN TING			WILLIAM E. MORRIS
REPRESENTATIVE IN CONGRESS VOTE FOR ONE (1)	Write In	DENNIS SPIVACK	MICHAEL N. CASTLE	MICHAEL BERG	KAREN M. HARTLEY-	
ATTORNEY GENERAL VOTE FOR ONE (1)	Write In	JOSEPH R. BIDEN, III	FERRIS WHARTON			
STATE TREASURER VOTE FOR ONE (1)	Write In	JACK MARKELL	ESTHELDA R. PARKER SELBY			
AUDITOR OF ACCOUNTS VOTE FOR ONE (1)	Write In	MICHAEL JOHN DALTO	R. THOMAS WAGNER, JR.			
STATE SENATOR DISTRICT 1 VOTE FOR ONE (1)	Write In	HARRIS B. McDOWELL, III	GREGORY T. CHAMBERS		TYLER PATRICK NIXON	
STATE REPRESENTATIVE DISTRICT 1 VOTE FOR ONE (1)	Write In	DENNIS P. WILLIAMS				
REGISTER OF WILLS VOTE FOR ONE (1)	Write In	DIANE CLARKE STREETT	JAMES ANTHONY			
RECORDER OF DEEDS VOTE FOR ONE (1)	Write In	MICHAEL E. ROZKOWSKI, SR.	JASON J. HORTIZ			
COUNTY COUNCIL DISTRICT 4 VOTE FOR ONE (1)	Write In	PENROSE HOLLINS				
SHERIFF VOTE FOR ONE (1)	Write In	MICHAEL P. WALSH	ALAN RHOADS			

AFTER MAKING ALL OF YOUR SELECTIONS, CAST YOUR BALLOT BY PUSHING THE GREEN "VOTE" BUTTON LOCATED BELOW THIS NOTICE.

BALLOT STYLE 001

Figure 3.2: Sample Office Bloc Ballot

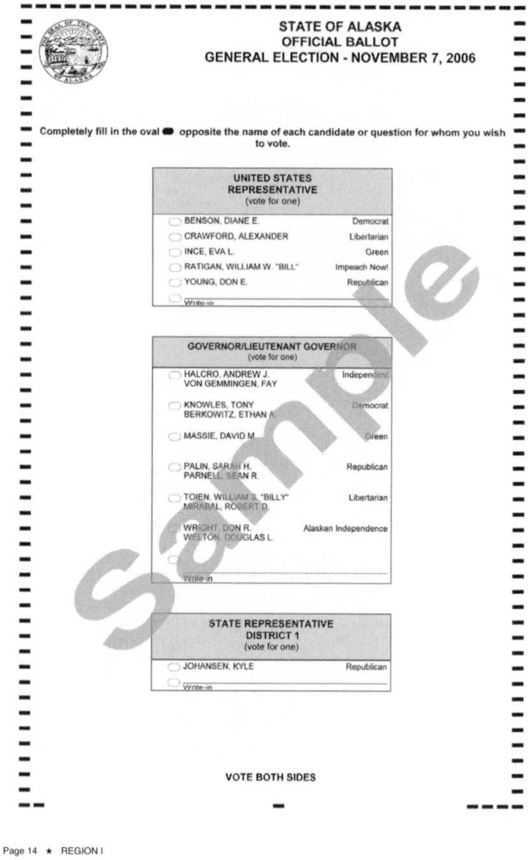

STATE OF ALASKA
OFFICIAL BALLOT
GENERAL ELECTION - NOVEMBER 7, 2006

Completely fill in the oval ● opposite the name of each candidate or question for whom you wish
to vote.

UNITED STATES REPRESENTATIVE
(vote for one)

○	BENSON, DIANE E.	Democrat
○	CRAWFORD, ALEXANDER	Libertarian
○	INCE, EVA L.	Green
○	RATIGAN, WILLIAM W. "BILL"	Impeach Now!
○	YOUNG, DON E.	Republican
○	Write-in	

GOVERNOR/LIEUTENANT GOVERNOR
(vote for one)

○	HALCRO, ANDREW J. VON GEMMINGEN, FAY	Independent
○	KNOWLES, TONY BERKOWITZ, ETHAN A.	Democrat
○	MASSIE, DAVID M.	Green
○	PALIN, SARAH H. PARNELL, SEAN R.	Republican
○	TOIEN, WILLIAM S. "BILLY" MIRABAL, ROBERT D.	Libertarian
○	WRIGHT, DON R. WELTON, DOUGLAS L.	Alaskan Independence
○		
	Write-in	

STATE REPRESENTATIVE DISTRICT 1
(vote for one)

○	JOHANSEN, KYLE	Republican
○	Write-in	

VOTE BOTH SIDES

made outright fraud much more difficult. Additionally, adoption of the Australian ballot should have had a considerable effect on the personal vote, the incumbency advantage, candidate emergence, and the impact of candidate quality on election outcomes. Secrecy at the polling place removed voters from the gaze of party workers and likely made it easier for them to choose their most preferred candidates. At the same time, having a single ballot listing all candidates for each office made it less conspicuous for voters to submit a split ticket. Once voters could more easily cast split-ballots, candidates and parties had an incentive to campaign more as individuals and less as teams. As a result, voters were able to punish or reward individual office holders without necessarily punishing their party's other candidates.

This decoupling of congressional elections and other offices on the ballot combined with the declining practice of rotation in office gave incumbents an increased opportunity to cultivate a personal vote. With the ability to develop a personal connection with voters, members were more likely to pursue representational strategies that would help maintain their place in the chamber. In fact, Katz and Sala (1996) maintain that House members quickly adapted their behavior inside the chamber in response to the new electoral situation. Specifically, they attribute an increase in committee assignment stability and development of the property rights norm with respect to committee assignments directly to the adoption of the Australian ballot. In conjunction with increasing tenure in office (Polsby 1968), legislators found that maintaining their placement on respective committees allowed them to more easily engage in constituency service.

Our expectations concerning the effects of the Australian ballot on election outcomes are relatively straightforward. The new ballot type focused the attention of voters more on the individual candidates than party labels. As such, we expect the qualities of individual candidates to be enhanced in the minds and behavior of the voters. This trend towards candidate-centered elections was further reinforced by the candidates themselves as they began to focus their campaigns and legislative activities on enhancing their personal reputations rather than the collective reputation of the party. Accordingly, we would expect candidate attributes to more directly affect electoral outcomes after adoption of the Australian ballot. In fact, much of the literature to date has argued that *only* after the adoption of the Australian ballot would candidate attributes have affected election outcomes (Jacobson 2009).

We also expect the effects of the Australian ballot to be non-uniform across the different types of ballot employed by the states. The office bloc ballot, for instance, is the ballot type most likely to encourage voters to focus on candidates for individual offices as it organizes the ballot by office rather than party. In contrast, we contend that the party column ballot would be more likely to facilitate straight-party ticket voting given that the ballot more closely resembled the format of the original party ballot used throughout much of the nineteenth century by the party organizations and it organized the ballot by party.

The effect of the Australian ballot on candidate emergence and retirement decisions is less straightforward. On the one hand, by drawing the attention of voters to individual candidates, the Australian ballot allowed candidates to be competitive for offices even if their fellow partisans were weaker candidates or if the party was strongly disadvantaged in a particular year. On the other hand, however, the emphasis placed on individual candidates gave parties less of an incentive to recruit strong candidates for all offices on the ballot. As presidential and congressional outcomes became less intertwined, parties could be confident that a reverse coattail effect would not doom their candidates higher up the ticket (Engstrom and Kernell 2005).

The new ballot structure allowed incumbent members of the House to become more formidable candidates in their own right as they were able to develop institutions to enhance their reputations with their constituencies (Katz and Sala 1996). As a result, we would expect to see fewer high quality candidates emerge across the board as the quality of the overall ticket began to be less important to the party's fortunes. Likewise, we would expect to see the "scare off" effect of incumbency—that is the ability of an incumbent to deter a quality challenger from running—to be enhanced as incumbents became more adept at marshaling the resources of office for electoral gain.

In sum, we expect that the Australian ballot would enhance the effects of candidate quality on election outcomes, while at the same time reducing the incentives for high quality candidates to seek office. Combined, these two forces would result in a sharp reduction in competitive elections as ambitious politicians become less likely to run for seats where the risks of losing are higher, while incumbents are able to provide greater amounts of material benefits to their constituents, thus increasing their likelihood of getting reelected. This self-reinforcing feedback loop is believed to be a major component of the incumbency advantage in the U.S. House.

3.3 The Direct Primary and Candidate Behavior

Prior to the adoption of the direct primary by individual states, most party nominations were made by party conventions. These conventions were typically comprised of party operatives who were chosen as delegates in a party caucus style meeting. These caucuses varied considerably both in how much deliberation went into the selection of delegates and the type of instruction given to the delegates. Some caucuses simply consisted of balloting for delegates with no deliberation or instruction, while others were much more deliberate in nature. As immigration and the industrial revolution increased the urbanization of the U.S., however, a number of problems with the caucus-convention system came into sharp relief. These problems included a lack of participation by the masses in caucuses, poor logistics for conducting caucuses as the population grew, and the inability of parties to exercise proper control of appointed office holders. Additionally, Reynolds (2006) maintains that ambitious, "hustling" candidates sought to undermine the authority of conventions by conducting outright campaigns for nominations. Finally, the parties' declining ability to exert control over "spoils system" appointees led to calls for a means to insure more efficient delivery of services—especially in the rapidly expanding urban areas (Ware 2002).

The direct primary spread quickly across the states in the early decades of the twentieth century. Why was this the case? In addition to the problems with the status quo noted above, Ware (2002) argues that Australian ballot reform served as a "catalyst" for direct primary legislation. For most states and parties, the transition to the Australian ballot had been smooth and in some cases beneficial to party interests, so opposition was lower than expected. Additionally, by way of printing the official ballot, states had sanctioned the existence of political parties as organizations subject to state control rather than persisting as private entities. Reformers were bolstered by their success with Australian ballot and were confident that they could convince the public and state legislatures that reforms were needed and would not be seriously disruptive of party politics.[4]

Our interests here are in understanding how the adoption of the direct primary changed the decision calculi of strategic politicians and, in turn, election outcomes. The direct primary essentially "neutered" political parties. Without direct control over nominations, parties could no longer determine the identity, loyalty, or quality of candidates appearing on the ballots under their name. As such, they could no longer effectively offer insurance to losing candidates as the number of party controlled positions rapidly diminished throughout the country. The cartel-like system of nominations was transformed into a political market, where individual, strategic politicians had to now make their own determination as to whether seeking a particular elective office was a worthwhile venture. As we argued above, party control of nominations allowed parties to subsidize the costs of candidate entry. Without this subsidy in place, we expect to see the supply of high quality candidates in marginally competitive or non-competitive races decrease. At the same time, the inability of parties to regulate the emergence decisions of strategic candidates likely increased competition for seats that were easily winnable by the respective parties.

We expect this change to further entrench incumbent House members as their increased electoral prowess interacted with the decreased incentive for quality candidates to emerge. Combined with the Australian ballot, the direct primary gradually helped shift congressional elections from party-centered to more candidate-centered over time. We contend that these changes combined to reduce the power of parties to shape electoral outcomes, while at the same time stifling electoral competition. Without the subsidy for entry, many strategic politicians chose to forego marginally competitive races. The simple fact is that the market for candidate entry no longer supported the high level of competition that we had previously seen with party control of the electoral machinery.

3.4 Incumbency and Candidate Emergence in Modern Congressional Elections

Though the claims we made above are unique when applied to pre–World War II elections, it is certainly well covered ground for the post–World War II era. In their now classic study of challenger emergence in congressional elections, for instance, Jacobson and Kernell (1983) examine whether political candidates exhibit strategic behavior in deciding whether or not to seek office. Through an examination of aggregate patterns of candidates' career decisions, they speculate as to the underlying motivations for politicians' behavior. As their theory is premised on rational calculations, they argue that experienced candidates are more likely to run for the House when national and partisan conditions are more favorable with respect to their likelihood of success. Jacobson and Kernell test their theory of strategic behavior on data from the 1974, 1980, and 1982 congressional elections and find convincing evidence in support of their hypotheses concerning strategic politicians. Not only do they conclude that experienced challengers wait until circumstances are optimal before they decide to run, they also find that strategic politicians play a pivotal role in determining the results of both district-level elections and the overall partisan composition of Congress.

Jacobson (1989) offers additional support for the strategic politicians theory by testing it against congressional elections data from 1946 to 1986. Through his examination of elections data during this 40-year period, he finds that experienced challengers do not emerge arbitrarily. Rather, their likelihood of running varies with their perceived chance of winning. Indeed, Jacobson concludes that a greater proportion of experienced or quality candidates emerge when prospects appear favorable to their party. In support of his contention that experienced politicians act strategically, he recognizes that quality challengers are more likely to emerge when a seat is uncontested and they rely increasingly on an incumbent's prior margin of victory as an important cue in deciding whether or not to run. Additionally, an incumbent's involvement in a political scandal could also lead to a greater likelihood that an experienced challenger emerges in a given seat.

In an attempt to further discern challengers' motivations in running for Congress, Banks and Kiewiet (1989) examine the behavior of non-experienced or weak candidates who emerge to challenge incumbents. While they agree with Jacobson and Kernell (1983) concerning the deterrent effects of incumbency with respect to the emergence of experienced challengers, they seek to understand why incumbency does not have the same effect on weak challengers. As they point out, nearly all incumbents are challenged from one election to the next, usually by candidates lacking electoral or political experience. Through their analysis of congressional primary data from 1980 through 1984, Banks and Kiewiet conclude that weak challengers run against incumbents for the same reason that strong challengers are more likely to run in open seat contests—to maximize their probability of getting elected to Congress. Given that their chances of earning the nomination would be small in an open seat race when experienced candidates are more likely to run, they accept the next best alternative—challenging a sitting incumbent. Even though their chances of defeat in the fall election are high, political amateurs recognize that running against an incumbent affords them the best opportunity to win their party's nomination, especially since more experienced challengers are likely to stay out of the race absent favorable national or partisan conditions.[5]

In a similar vein, since the early 1970s, students of congressional politics have documented a fairly stable pattern with respect to elections in the U.S. House—the relatively high reelection rate of incumbents in Congress. Building upon the early work that first recognized the advantages accruing to incumbents (Erikson 1971; Ferejohn 1977; Mayhew 1974), several distinct explanations have been offered to account for the overwhelming rates at which incumbent legislators get reelected in the modern era. Initially, the incumbency advantage was attributed to institutional features such as legislative casework (Fiorina 1977), legislative activism (Johannes and McAdams 1981), advertising (Cover and Brumberg 1982), generational replacement among members (Alford and Hibbing 1981; Born 1979), and redistricting (Cover 1977; Erikson 1972). Others have suggested that the advantage can be explained by legislators' personal home styles in their districts (Fenno 1978), rational entry decisions by strategic candidates (Jacobson and Kernell 1983; Krasno 1994), the increasing costs of House campaigns (Abramowitz 1991), and a growing personal vote (Cain et al. 1987).

In their critique of the existing scholarly literature on the incumbency advantage, Gelman and King (1990) rigorously prove that many commonly used measures of the incumbency advantage—such as sophomore surge and retirement slump—produce biased and/or inconsistent estimates of the advantage. As a result, Gelman and King develop a technique that corrects for most of the inherent problems in measuring the incumbency advantage. In doing so, they find evidence of an incumbency advantage as early as the beginning of the twentieth century, as well as a large jump in the advantage accruing to incumbents in the mid-1960s. Drawing upon this new estimation technique, Cox and Katz (1996) re-examine why the incumbency advantage grew in the mid-1960s. Their model of the incumbency advantage is a refined version of the Gelman-King model that allows them to account for the differences in candidate quality between parties and the possibility that incumbents "scare off" high quality challengers. Although they consider alternative explanations for the growth in incumbency advantage during the modern era, they ultimately conclude that the growth was driven almost entirely by an increase in a quality effect (i.e., the advantage that incumbent legislators received from not facing an experienced challenger).

In more recent work, Cox and Katz (2002) provide the most comprehensive and succinct account of the incumbency advantage in the literature to date. Unlike other treatments of this subject, Cox and Katz find that the regularity of redistricting that resulted from the Supreme Court decision in *Wesberry v. Sanders* (1964) drove the large 1960s increase in the incumbency advantage. They find convincing evidence that the combination of liberal leaning judges and Democratically-controlled state legislatures drew new district boundaries that efficiently spread Democratic voters across districts in a way that maximized the share of seats Democrats could expect to control in the House, while simultaneously creating extremely safe seats for the remaining Republican members. When considering the incumbency advantage, Cox and Katz offer two distinct conclusions: (1) the mid-1960s redistricting created a larger incumbency advantage for Republicans that explains the explosive growth of the incumbency advantage in the 1960s; and (2) they maintain that the regularity of redistricting following *Wesberry* created an environment whereby quality challengers and incumbents avoided facing each other as much as possible.

3.4.1 Are Modern Theories Time Bound?

We believe the contemporary theories of congressional elections discussed above can also help explain the dynamics of pre–World War II elections. Yet, we also recognize that to undertake work across historical eras, we need to consider the potential confounds attributed to systemic structural changes over time. Despite the differences in how elections were conducted, we argue there is reason to believe that late nineteenth and early twentieth century politicians would be affected by similar strategic parameters such as likelihood of victory, value of the seat, and opportunity costs that are faced by modern day candidates. Indeed, there is no reason to suspect that individual ambition would be tempered by varying electoral institutions—regardless of whether prospective candidates have to seek the approval of the party machine or emerge through a direct primary—the goal is to run when one can maximize the probability of victory (Kernell 1977; Rohde 1979; Schlesinger 1966). In fact, we contend that the dramatic institutional changes that occurred over time are the linchpin of our study in that they allow us to draw inferences about the effects of electoral institutions that simply cannot be undertaken with either modern or historical data in isolation.

Given the strategic parallels between modern elections and those in our historical elections data set, we think the strategic politicians theory—as posited by Jacobson and Kernell (1983)—is applicable in this historical context. We also believe that the data on candidates we have collected offers us leverage in examining changing patterns in the incumbency advantage back to the late nineteenth century. We know, for instance, the size of the incumbency advantage has varied over time. Through a series of analyses, we hope to be able to speak to these changes and examine the relationship to institutional changes as outlined above. Ultimately, for congressional elections theories to "travel" back to the pre–World War II era, we must demonstrate that the conventional view of historical elections is incomplete and that candidates and parties responded to strategic incentives much like they do today.

3.5 Old Evidence and New Arguments

We readily concede that the mechanics of congressional elections in the modern era and the electoral environment from earlier eras are different (Bensel 2004; Summers 2004; Ware 2002). Nevertheless, we contend that the dynamics facing congressional candidates prior to the emergence of a candidate-centered system are more similar to those faced by modern day candidates than previously recognized. For example, we have found evidence that experienced politicians did behave strategically in a subset of elections across the late nineteenth and early twentieth centuries (Carson and Roberts 2005). More specifically, we demonstrated that much like in the modern era, candidates with previous electoral experience were more successful at securing votes and were more likely to seek office when national and/or local conditions favored their candidacy. Moreover, factors such as national economic conditions, an incumbent with a small prior electoral margin, and the presence of an open seat were all related to experienced candidates' entry decisions. These are effects that we would expect to observe in the contemporary era characterized by candidate-centered elections, but do not necessarily correspond with the conventional view of elections during the late nineteenth century.

Our expectations regarding the preceding argument build upon an extensive literature demonstrating that nineteenth and early twentieth century representatives (and the party organizations that selected them) responded rationally to changes in their incentive structure when deciding to run for reelection in Congress (Aldrich 1995; Brady et al. 1999b; Fiorina et al. 1975; Kernell 1977, 2003; Price 1975). While there were clear differences in elections then as compared to the modern era, this does not mean that members failed to respond to the incentive system in place at the time. Kernell (1977), for instance, considers the effects of three primary factors and their impact on nineteenth century congressional careers—ambition, competition, and rotation. More specifically, Kernell (1977, 690) argues that the membership in Congress began to stabilize by the late nineteenth century since electoral competitiveness was gradually beginning to decline as a result of institutional changes such as the 1896 realignment, ballot reform, and the adoption of the direct primary. Over time, these changes led to longer tenure in Congress since incumbents were less likely to be deterred from seeking reelection.

Building upon Kernell's (1977) argument, Brady et al. (1999b, 507-508) maintain that careerism in Congress began earlier than previous accounts have suggested—well before the turn of the century. They conclude that different factors influenced whether incumbents sought reelection as well as their electoral viability if they ran. In their words, "Careerism, as a behavioral characteristic of incumbents, is independent (or, at least, distinct from) electoral safety." Furthermore, as the size of the federal government grew and the power of congressional committees steadily began to increase, the value of staying in the House and making a career out of legislative politics also increased.[6] Over time, this contributed to a marked decline in voluntary turnover in the House as a greater number of legislators began seeking reelection to more than one or two terms of office.

Beyond the preceding arguments, there is a growing amount of anecdotal and scholarly evidence that nineteenth century legislators were affected by some form of an "electoral connection" with respect to their career and legislative decisions. Mayhew (1974), in his classic formulation, argues that the singular desire to get reelected forces members of Congress to remain responsive to their constituents. Although it is unclear whether Mayhew's argument concerning legislative behavior applies outside of the contemporary era, there has been some speculation that the fear of retrospective punishment by the voters might be equally applicable, albeit to a more limited extent, across time.[7] In

discussing the potential applicability of Mayhew's formulation during
an era of high turnover rates in Congress, for instance, Charles Stewart
III (1989, 9–10) argues that:

> [T]he extent of the nineteenth-century congressional revolv-
> ing door has frequently been over-interpreted. The high
> turnover rates mask the extent to which late-nineteenth and
> early-twentieth century MCs were professional politicians,
> but politicians with a higher priority on local careers than
> on national ones. Thus, the "election pursuit" hypothesis
> that drives current congressional research in this tradition
> can be applied to past congressional behavior if the con-
> ceptualization of election pursuit is made more general,
> allowing for a broader notion of what MCs wanted to do
> with their future careers.

As further support for this argument, several scholars have found
limited evidence of an "electoral connection" prior to the adoption
of the Australian ballot. Bianco, Spence, and Wilkerson (1996), for
instance, examine passage of the Compensation Act of 1816 to investigate whether additional evidence could be marshaled to confirm the
existence of an electoral connection in the antebellum era. As Bianco
et al. (1996, 147) suggest, "It is one thing to argue that a congressional
career was less attractive or less feasible in an earlier time than it is
today, but another to conclude that members of the early Congress
were unconcerned about the electoral consequences of their behavior."
They chose to focus on the congressional pay raise passed in 1816
since this type of legislation would be more likely to yield observable
electoral consequences. In their analysis, they find that legislators
who were more electorally vulnerable were less likely to support the
legislative compensation plan and that representatives who chose to
support the plan were less likely to seek reelection, due to the apparent
electoral risks of such action. Based on their results, Bianco et al.
(1996, 167–168) conclude that:

> Conventional wisdom has it that contemporary notions
> of the electoral connection cannot be applied to the early
> Congress. Our analysis ... suggests that an electoral con-
> nection may have operated in the early Congress as well.
> That the Compensation Act was unusually controversial
> and clearly an exception to the normal politics of the period

is not in question. The point is that the conventional wisdom sees no role for the electoral connection in any analysis of the early Congress. Did an electoral connection operate in the early Congress? The contribution of this paper is to move the conventional wisdom from answering "no, never" to saying "perhaps on occasion."

More recently, Carson and Engstrom (2005) take up the challenge posed by Bianco et al. (1996) by examining whether other events in the nineteenth century might suggest evidence of an electoral connection during that era. Specifically, they propose a test of the electoral connection in early American politics by investigating the electoral aftershocks of the disputed presidential election of 1824. Using newly available county-level presidential voting data, along with the unique circumstances associated with the presidential contest, they examine the connection between representative behavior, district public opinion, and electoral outcomes. Carson and Engstrom (2005) find that representatives that voted for John Quincy Adams in the House contest, yet were from districts supporting Andrew Jackson, were targeted for ouster and suffered a substantial vote-loss in the subsequent midterm election. They also find that the entry of a quality challenger had a sizable impact on the fortunes of incumbent legislators, decades before any prior evidence of this type of effect. Their results serve to confirm the presence of an electoral connection and representative accountability during this historical era.

To be clear, we are not questioning that the importance of strategic politicians and the emergence of candidate-centered politics are related for the post–World War II era. Rather, we think there is good reason to suspect a similar pattern of strategic behavior across different eras, even when the party organizations controlled the electoral machinery. Thus, while we may see patterns of strategic behavior in keeping with modern theories of electoral politics, we think the mechanism through which this behavior occurs is the strategic calculation of ambitious politicians and parties and is not necessarily a function of candidate-centered campaigns. As discussed earlier, political parties have an incentive to maximize the quality of candidates running under their label at all times, but should have an easier time convincing experienced candidates to seek election when the combination of national and local conditions made success more likely. Regardless of whether prospective candidates have to seek the approval of the party machine or run on their own via a direct primary, the goal is to run when one can maximize the probability of victory (Carson and Roberts 2005; Kernell 1977). Further, prior to the advent of the direct primary, political parties could prevent weak candidates from seeking election under the party label—once the direct primary took hold, the parties lost this ability. In fact, as we show later, we see more experienced challengers in a party-centered era due to the fact that parties had nearly absolute control over the ballots.

Available evidence on the role of congressional campaign committees in the nineteenth century (Kolodny 1998) further suggests that political parties understood the importance of congressional elections, especially with respect to the impact on the institutional makeup of Congress. In her authoritative account from this era, Kolodny argues persuasively that party leaders in Congress established and maintained congressional campaign committees as early as the 1860s in order to control and disseminate information about party positions and to prevent being subsumed by the president in national campaigns. This latter point in particular is reflected in Kolodny's (1998) discussion of the rationale for organizing congressional campaign committees. She points out that the idea that all party candidates would unite under the presidential campaign was short-lived. As early as 1866, House Republicans organized a committee to further their electoral goals in the upcoming midterm elections. In short, the differing constituency bases made a single campaign committee unworkable.

Kolodny's research also suggests that the presence of high profile party leaders on congressional campaign committees points toward their importance as mechanisms to attain majority status through their role in recruiting and campaigning for individual House candidates. She maintains that party elites were in an ideal position to recruit quality candidates and encourage them to emerge when conditions were most favorable for both the candidates and the party organization. Moreover, Kolodny (1998, 47) notes that House speaker Joseph Cannon (Republican–IL) went on the road prior to the 1904 elections to campaign for House candidates in "doubtful" districts, with the Republicans eventually winning all but one of the seats that Cannon visited. Kolodny maintains that the increasing literacy rate among the electorate led to a change in campaign style as voters began to demand information rather than "flowery oratory." It is certainly plausible that increasingly literate and informed voters would be impacted by the quality of the campaign messenger, and unlikely that party leaders such as Cannon would undergo such an arduous task as canvassing the countryside for congressional candidates if national conditions were the primary determinant of election outcomes.

Kolodny's observation about voters is another important factor worth noting in seeking to understand the transformation in electoral politics during this era. The nature of the American electorate was clearly evolving during the late nineteenth and early twentieth centuries. In contrast to the popular conception of voting behavior at this time, there is considerable evidence suggesting that voters were cognizant of individual politicians and were not simply casting blind votes based on partisan tickets. In describing patterns of voting behavior from this era, Silbey (1991, 174) maintains that campaigns served to "rouse" the public with individuals frequently and openly discussing vote choice with their neighbors. The regular discussion of politics among voters led them to pay much closer attention to the specific details of campaigns. Indeed, the available evidence suggests that they expected to be informed by candidates prior to the election and regularly went to the polls. Indeed, Silbey's argument suggests that much like politics today, voter turnout was considerably higher among individuals with greater levels of wealth and education.

Anecdotal accounts suggest that voters from this era did not have to process copious amounts of information about the positions of candidates. Instead, they simply chose the correct party ballot and dropped it in the box. The differences in turnout give us reason to question this conventional wisdom, however. Modern theories of voter turnout suggest that the wealthy and educated vote at higher rates because it is easier for them to acquire information about candidates (Rosenstone and Hansen 1993). If differences in information costs had an effect on turnout during this era, perhaps voters were not simply responding to party labels as previously believed. Indeed, Kleppner (1983) has analyzed party activity in the West and demonstrates that voting on party cues was not universal throughout the country. He maintains that traditional party cleavages did not fit the Western states, so most voters never developed a firm attachment to any political party. He estimates that less than two-thirds of Western voters were repeat voters for the same party from election to election.

Based on the preceding discussion, we contend that a more careful reading of history suggests that the electorate may have been more responsive to individual candidates than previously believed. As the influence of party organizations began to gradually decline following major institutional reforms (i.e., the widespread adoption of the Australian ballot and direct primaries across the states), this may have contributed to declining voter participation as well given the reduced input by the parties. As the influence of parties over elections declined over time, their ability to bring voters to the polls may have been reduced as well.

Our discussion about congressional elections in the late nineteenth and early twentieth centuries has important implications for our understanding of politics during this era. As the expansive literature on the historical development of the U.S. Congress demonstrates, a great deal has been learned about legislative behavior, organization, and policy making by studying these developments across time. While much additional work in this vein remains to be done, one area that has received substantially less attention is how the electoral politics of the congressional institution have shaped the historical and institutional development of Congress. Indeed, we would argue that American *electoral* development underlies many of the institutional changes that have occurred in Congress. The adoption of the Australian ballot, the appearance of direct primaries, the role of parties in recruiting candidates, the growth of the incumbency advantage accruing to legislators, and the emergence of a candidate-centered electoral system are all important historical events shaping Congress in one way or another. By studying these changes in the context of nineteenth and twentieth century congressional elections, we and others who build upon our work can shed further light on the question of how the transformation in electoral politics directly impacts the institutional development of Congress.

Beyond learning more about historic elections and their impact on institutional changes in Congress, a more systematic analysis of congressional elections during this era will also yield notable implications for our ability to test the robustness of contemporary theories of electoral politics in a largely unexplored historical context. If the electoral milieu between the historical and modern eras is not as different as previously believed, then we can gain important analytical leverage by examining unanswered questions across time. If nineteenth and early twentieth century candidates were responding to "traditional" indicators of national forces, were they also responding to other factors? How did the declining role of political parties in congressional elections over time affect electoral competition? We argue that examining electoral data across a longer time span offers us increased leverage in evaluating important electoral changes and developments. It also allows us to test the applicability of contemporary theories of electoral politics in a very different historical context. If our theories of contemporary phenomena are truly generalizable, then they should be applicable across time.

In the remainder of the book, we bring data to bear on the empirical questions and hypotheses raised in this chapter. We begin with some more descriptive trends to highlight some of the behavioral patterns of strategic politicians during the pre–World War II era. Next, we turn to more systematic analysis to understand when, and under what conditions, strategic politicians choose to emerge in these races. Lastly, we examine factors influencing both why and how incumbents are reelected to Congress over time. We then conclude by discussing a number of implications from our analyses.

4

Exploring Historic and Modern Election Trends

One of the biggest challenges to testing modern theories in any historical context is the difficulty of finding the necessary data to systematically evaluate the theories of interest. Until fairly recently, such historical tests were impractical due to a lack of readily available data, the labor-intensive nature of the data collection process, and the resources required to undertake such an endeavor. Recent developments in electronic archiving and historical research, however, have made it possible for us to gather the data necessary to examine the issues and questions pertaining to changes in electoral competitiveness over time. As such, we can now begin to examine more systematically factors contributing to the decline in competitiveness in U.S. House races over time, the impact and emergence of strategic politicians in light of electoral reforms, and the growth in the incumbency advantage for sitting House members.

We have chosen to examine elections to the U.S. House of Representatives held in the late nineteenth and early twentieth centuries to systematically test our central research questions.[1] This, in effect, allows us to determine whether the quality of candidates directly affected election results and predict when, and under what conditions, experienced candidates are likely to run for office. Data on district-level congressional results and candidate identification information have recently become available for this period with the publishing of *United States Congressional Elections, 1788–1997: The Official Results*, by far the most comprehensive source for electoral data since the founding of our nation (Dubin 1998). From this, one can code relevant information on the names of the incumbent and related challengers, the vote totals

56

on which percentages of the two-party vote were computed, as well as partisan affiliation for each congressional candidate. These latter data can be supplemented with information contained in Martis (1989) to fill gaps in partisan affiliation for House candidates.

To illustrate the changes in candidate and party success in the House over time, Figure 4.1 displays the percent of Democrats, Republicans, and third party members serving in Congress from 1873 to 2009. One pattern immediately evident from the figure is that the percentage of third party members during this era was exceptionally small. There is no single Congress in this period where the proportion of third party legislators exceeds 8 percent. After the turn of the twentieth century, the percentage of third party members declines even further, averaging only about 1 percent through the early 2000s. Prior to the turn of the twentieth century, we also observe considerable electoral volatility, where neither major political party had a distinct, sustained advantage in majority status due to the greater upheaval from one election to the next. Over time, however, this pattern gradually begins to change as extended periods of one-party majority control become more frequent in the House. Except for a few congresses during the 1910s, for instance, the Republicans controlled a majority of seats in the U.S. House from the 54th to the 72nd Congresses. After the 1930 midterm elections shifted the electoral fortunes of the Republicans due to the growing economic depression, the Democrats became the new majority party in Congress and retained control of the House for nearly the next 60 years. At the same time, the variation in the percentage of seats controlled by either party was significantly reduced in the post–World War II period.

Once we had coded the election returns for all congressional candidates during this era, we were able to turn our attention to documenting several noteworthy patterns and trends in the data, especially those pertaining to changes in incumbency reelection and strategic candidate emergence. Figure 4.2 examines one such pattern by focusing on the proportion of incumbents that were reelected from 1872–2008. This figure clearly shows that the incumbent reelection rate for House members has steadily increased over the full range of elections that we analyze. This pattern is especially interesting for two reasons. First, the average reelection rate for incumbents from 1872–1944 is 84 percent, a figure that is much higher than we might expect given the general electoral volatility in this era. In fact, in election years such as 1900, 1904, 1908, 1916, and 1944, the reelection rates of incumbents approached or were slightly higher than 90 percent, a pattern much

Figure 4.1: Percent of Members by Party Affiliation, 1873–2009

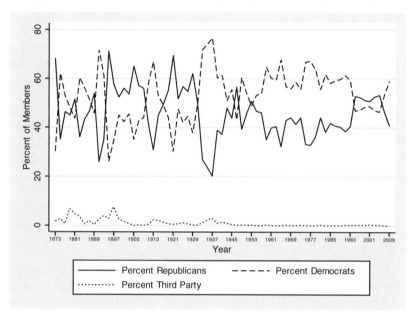

more reflective of elections in the contemporary era. Second, the re-election rate for incumbents steadily grew after World War II. Indeed, the average incumbency reelection rate from 1946–2008 is 94 percent. Clearly, the trend displayed in this figure warrants further attention in that it suggests that much of our understanding of the incumbency advantage across time is either incomplete or incorrect—on this point, see especially Alford and Brady (1989).

Another pattern reflected in Figure 4.2 is a significant amount of volatility in incumbent reelection rates during the pre–World War II era. For instance, an examination of the patterns in the figure shows that the percentage of incumbents reelected in this period ranged from a low of 63 percent in 1874 to a high of 96 percent in 1944. In contrast, the range in the percentage of incumbents reelected during the post–war era resides in a much tighter band between 82 and 99 percent.[2] The volatility displayed in this figure seems to reflect a strong correlation between economic conditions and incumbent reelection (Lynch 2002). For example, the low reelection rate in 1874 is likely the result of a

Figure 4.2: Reelection Rates for Incumbents, 1872–2008

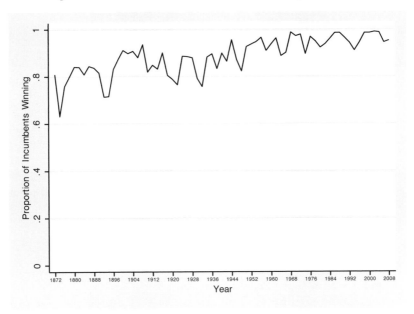

general backlash against incumbents stemming from the Panic of 1873. A similar pattern seems to have occurred in both 1892 and 1894, the latter most likely a function of the widespread economic depression which began a year earlier in 1893. Although not as pronounced in magnitude, we see similar declines in the 1922 midterm election following the so-called "Do Nothing" Sixty-seventh Congress, and again in 1932 when Democrat Franklin Delano Roosevelt defeated Republican incumbent president Herbert Hoover in a landslide presidential election during the Great Depression.

If we examine the proportion of incumbents getting reelected by party, we observe a number of additional and noteworthy patterns in the data. As Figure 4.3 shows, there is considerable volatility in reelection rates for incumbents from both parties in the pre–World War II era. Nevertheless, we see that incumbent Democrats generally seem to get reelected at a higher rate than Republicans in many elections across the entire time period. This pattern is at least partially explained by the fact that Democrats dominated elections in most Southern states during much of this period. Whereas there are only five or six elections prior to World War II where more than 90 percent of incumbent Republicans are reelected, incumbent Democrats win at rates higher than 90 percent in almost a third of the elections from this period. When we shift our attention to electoral losses as reflected by the proportion of incumbents reelected, several elections stand out. Without a doubt, 1874 and 1932 were clearly bad years for Republicans, with only about 55 percent of Republican incumbents reelected in these separate elections.[3] For Democrats, 1894 is easily the worst election in our sample, with nearly 40 percent of incumbents who sought reelection being defeated.[4] Not surprisingly, all three elections were preceded by severe economic recessions that appear to have challenged the majority party's hold on Congress. In the post–war era, 1948, 1964, and 1974 stand out for Republican losses, even though more than 70 percent of Republican Party incumbents managed to win reelection in each of these years.

An alternative way to think about incumbent safety is to examine the average incumbent vote by election year in the U.S. House. In Figure 4.4, we see that there has been a gradual increase in the average incumbent vote percentage over time.[5] Whereas the average vote percentage hovered between 56 and 62 percent during the first two decades of our analysis, there was a sharp increase following the 1892 elections. After another increase around 1904, the average incumbent vote declined for several elections in the early part of the twentieth century before increasing again to the highest percentages in the 1922 and 1926 midterm elections (both around 67 percent). Over the next two decades, we observe another sharp decline in average incumbent vote culminating in the 1934 midterm elections, before a gradual increase over the next few election cycles. Finally, we see a gradual increase again starting in the 1950s, which has remained fairly steady (save for the early 1990s) and has been the subject of much prior research (see, e.g., Cox and Katz 1996).

When we separate out the preceding figure by incumbent party affiliation, we observe a very different pattern across the two parties. As Figure 4.5 suggests, incumbent Democrats appear to win at slightly higher margins than incumbent Republicans in most of the elections in our sample. In certain elections (e.g., 1890, 1910, 1922, 1932, 1948, 1958, 1974, and 2006) the difference in average incumbent vote between the parties is at least 10 percentage points. The average incumbent vote for Republicans fluctuates around 60 percent during the entire

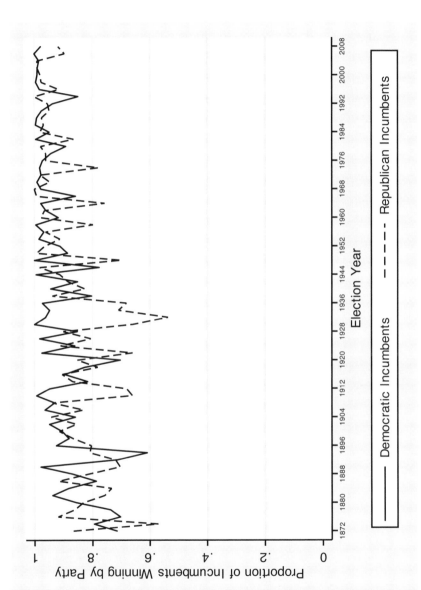

Figure 4.3: Incumbent Reelection Rate by Party, 1872–2008

Figure 4.4: Average House Incumbent Vote, 1872–2008

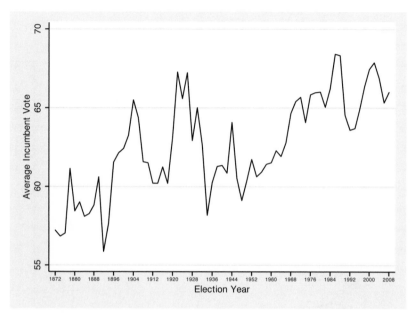

period of our analysis (until around 1980), but for Democrats it is closer to 70 percent. This is not surprising given the trend reported earlier in Figure 4.1, which suggested that the Republicans were the more dominant party during much of the late nineteenth and early twentieth centuries. Based on the pattern in this figure, it would seem as though incumbent Republicans often are considered *marginal* (at least by contemporary standards), whereas incumbent Democrats appear to be winning, on average, by much larger vote percentages. Some of this pattern can be explained by the Democrats' one party dominance in the South, but not all of it, as many Democratic held seats in the South went uncontested and hence are not included in this figure. What most likely accounts for this difference between the parties is the Republicans' use of efficient gerrymanders during the late nineteenth century (Engstrom 2006).

Figure 4.5: Average House Incumbent Vote by Party, 1872–2008

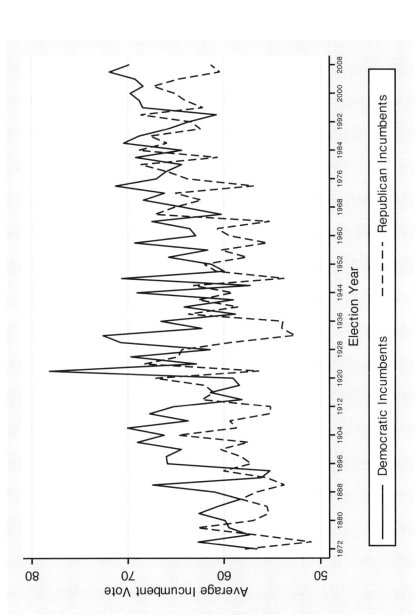

4.1 Candidate Quality Data

Compiling House election returns and partisan affiliation for members was relatively straightforward. Less straightforward was the coding and collection of information on candidate quality or experience. Throughout our analysis, we measure candidate quality as whether or not a candidate currently holds or has previously held elective office. While other, more nuanced, measures exist, we chose not to employ them for two specific reasons. First, and most importantly, almost all studies have demonstrated that the simple dichotomy performs as well as more sophisticated measures in other studies of challenger quality (Jacobson 2009). As a result, the dichotomous measure of quality gives us a more parsimonious model without losing important substantive information. Second, it would be extremely difficult to construct a scale measure that would compare the "quality" of previous offices held in this time period where the range and responsibilities of previous offices held is much greater than during the modern era. That is, while the simple dichotomy is a blunt and imprecise measure of candidate quality, we think that constructing a more nuanced measure for this time period may increase measurement error for some offices, while providing very little additional precision in other cases.

Unfortunately, traditional sources of candidate quality data in the contemporary era such as the *CQ Weekly Report* and Project Vote Smart are not available for the era under examination. Nevertheless, we have confirmed that many of these data can be collected from other sources. In particular, our efforts to identify data on candidates' political backgrounds were facilitated by the use of the *Biographical Directory of the U.S. Congress, 1774 to Present*.[6] This web site provides relevant experiential data for congressional incumbents who served during this historical era, challengers who defeated incumbents, and challengers who went on to serve in either the House or Senate prior to or after the election in question. Using this source alone, one can often find relevant background data on approximately 50 percent of the candidates running for election to a given Congress.

Beyond the biographical directory of members of Congress, another useful web site for locating background data is The Political Graveyard.[7] This site currently contains historical data on over 217,000 politicians, including their political experience and where they are buried. While much of our data were located from these two main sources, we also utilized *The New York Times* Historical Index, Google, various state historical societies, and archival research of state and local newspapers (employing Ancestry.com) to find supplementary background data on candidates who ran for Congress during this political era. We were also able to locate a number of biographical directories of state legislators (both online and print versions) to help us fill in existing gaps in our candidate background data over this period.[8] The closer our examination took us to the contemporary era, the greater proportion of cases of candidate quality we were able to track down using these combined sources.

Prior research has demonstrated that collecting data on candidate political experience is both practical and worthwhile. Indeed, our search efforts in this regard have yielded somewhat surprising results with respect to candidate experience when compared directly to trends in the modern era. Looking at Figure 4.6, for instance, we see that roughly 40–50 percent of both Democratic and Republican incumbents faced a quality challenger during the latter part of the nineteenth century—more than twice the average that we regularly observe today in congressional races. Moreover, we begin to see a sharp decline in the percentage of experienced candidates running against incumbents of either party at the turn of the century, most likely a function of changing electoral laws occurring during this period. Indeed, this decline in the proportion of experienced candidates facing off against incumbents coincides almost perfectly with the adoption of the Australian ballot and direct primaries near the turn of the century.

Beginning in the early twentieth century and continuing until the end of World War II, we observe a relatively stable period in experienced candidate entry decisions (with only a few exceptions). We also begin to see an increase in the proportion of incumbents facing a quality challenger—especially among Republicans—around 1950, although this pattern begins to subside by the end of the century. Two elections in particular stand out—both 1974 and 1982—where the proportion of Republican incumbents facing Democratic challengers exceeds 40 percent. Overall, the proportion of incumbents facing a quality challenger declined by more than 50 percent from 1872 to 1944, before increasing somewhat during the next six decades.

When we consider the evidence from Figure 4.6 in conjunction with the preceding figures examining reelection rates for incumbents, an interesting picture emerges regarding incumbent success. As discussed earlier, 1874 was clearly a bad year for Republican House incumbents. When we view this election in the context of the evidence in the figure,

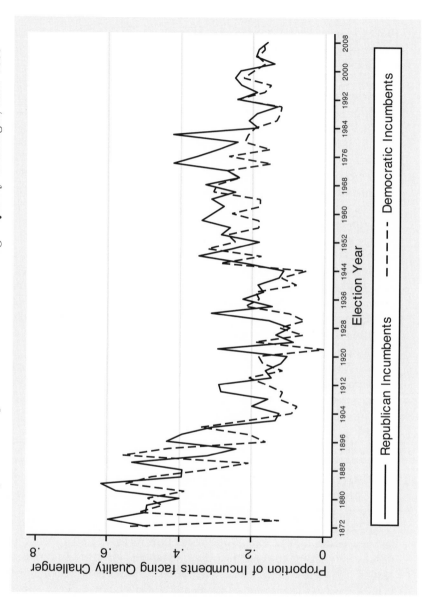

Figure 4.6: Proportion of Incumbents Facing a Quality Challenger, 1872–2008

we can see why—approximately 60 percent of Republican incumbents in this election faced an experienced challenger. A similar pattern holds in the 1884 election, although the proportion of incumbent Democrats facing an experienced challenger was almost as high. Among Democrats, 1892 and 1894 were watershed elections, as between 45 and 55 percent of incumbent Democrats faced a quality challenger in these two elections. In the early part of the twentieth century, we see that the proportion of incumbents facing quality challengers in both parties declined considerably, although there are still a few elections—1912, 1922, and 1932—where roughly a third of all Republican incumbents faced an experienced opponent. We observe a few additional election years after World War II where the proportion of Republicans facing a quality challenger averaged between 30 and 40 percent, including 1948, 1958, 1964, 1968, 1974, and 1982. Not surprisingly, these are all years in which Republican incumbents were significantly less likely to be reelected.

In focusing more specifically on candidates seeking office during this period, it is interesting to examine the candidates who ran for a seat in the House, but were unsuccessful in their attempts. Many of these losing candidates lacked prior electoral experience, which is exactly the type of pattern we would expect to find in the contemporary era rather than during this specific period in history based on conventional accounts of late nineteenth and early twentieth century elections. As noted in Chapter 2, the party organizations largely controlled access to the ballots during the late nineteenth century and the quality of individual candidates was supposed to matter little, if at all, during this era. With the adoption of the Australian ballot and the emergence of the direct primary at the turn of the century, there were seemingly greater opportunities for voters to split their tickets in order to selectively reward or punish incumbents.

When we investigate this phenomenon in more detail, we uncover some rather compelling evidence about the effects of quality on election outcomes. For instance, the results in Figure 4.7 clearly demonstrate that incumbents who faced candidates lacking prior elective experience had a much higher chance of winning than those running against candidates with elective experience, especially prior to 1956. When facing a non-quality challenger, 92.2 percent of House incumbents on average win prior to 1946 (with a range of 81.6 to 98.8 percent). In contrast, only 61.4 percent of incumbents on average win when forced to compete against a quality opponent in this era (with a much greater

Figure 4.7: Proportion of Incumbents Winning by Challenger Type, 1872–2008

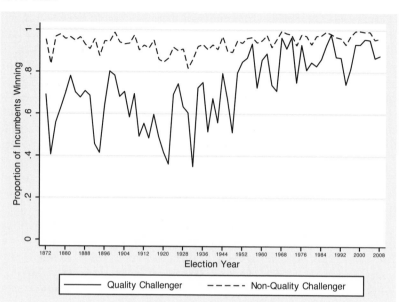

range of 34.9 to 80.3 percent). The average difference in probability of success across challenger type prior to 1946, then, is 31 percent.

By comparison, an average of 96 percent of House incumbents facing a non-quality opponent won during the post–World War II period. For those facing a quality challenger, however, 85 percent of incumbents on average still managed to win during this period. Although initially surprising, there are a couple of potential explanations for this development. It may be the case, for instance, that the difference between quality and non-quality is not as important as it once was. A more likely explanation, however, is that incumbents during the post–war era have gotten better at deciding when to run or retire (i.e., when they suspect that their chances of winning will be greater). Based on these preliminary trends, it would appear that candidate experience had a pronounced effect on election outcomes as far back as the late nineteenth and early twentieth centuries. We investigate these patterns more systematically in Chapters 5 and 6.

So what was the primary occupation(s) of candidates during this period in history? As is common in the modern era, many successful candidates for the U.S. House previously served in another elective office prior to their first election to the chamber. A fairly large percentage of quality candidates who went on to serve in the House in this era had previously served as either state representatives or senators, many for several years prior to their initial run for the House. Others served as current or former governors, city mayors, elected judges, city council members, or aldermen. At times, former members of either the U.S. House or Senate would sit out one or more terms and then seek the nomination again to the House—of which many managed to win at least one additional term.[9] For those running for office without elective or political experience, the most common occupations were lawyers, businessmen, newspapermen, farmers, ministers, and even the occasional cowboy.

4.2 Missing Data on Candidate Quality

We were able to collect candidate-specific data for approximately 13,000 congressional races from 1872–1944. In Figure 4.8, we plot the percentage of cases for which we were able to identify background information for candidates running for office during this period. In some years, such as 1894 and 1934, we were able to identify background information for a relatively high proportion of candidates seeking office. Much of this success owed to the relatively high rates of turnover in these years, when a greater number of incumbents were defeated or a larger number of open seats than normal were present. In other years, like 1908 and 1916, we were somewhat less successful in uncovering information on candidates running for the House. Overall, we have successfully identified background data for nearly 77 percent of candidates running for office from 1872–1944. While this represents an enormous data collection effort, especially given the difficulty of tracking down candidate quality data across the era in question, one issue we have had to address was how to deal with the candidates for which we could not find background information.

We considered three possible methods of dealing with the missing data. The first approach would be to simply listwise delete the races for which we could not uncover challenger information. This approach, however, can lead to severe estimation bias since the missing cases are

Figure 4.8: Percentage of Candidate Background Data Found, 1872–1944

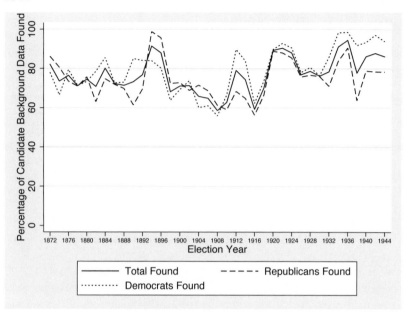

certainly not missing at random (King, Honaker, Joseph, and Scheve 2001). That is, we know that the missing cases never served in Congress nor attained prominent state or national positions. In those states for which we have historical legislative directories, we also know that these individual never served in the state legislature (a common stepping stone to running for the U.S. House). Thus, it is certainly more likely that the candidates for which we were unable to find background data were more likely to lack political experience.

A second approach for dealing with the missing data would be to employ the solution used by Jacobson (1989). In his analysis of strategic behavior from 1946–1986, he assumes that all the candidates for whom there is no background information are non-quality or lacked elective experience. This approach has the advantage of taking into account some of the information we know about the overall pool of candidates given the lack of information obtained after consulting a variety of different sources. Since we would be applying this distinction exclusively to losing candidates, however, there is the distinct possibility of biasing the results in support of our hypotheses.

In the end, we chose to impute the missing data using the multiple imputation approach developed by King et al. (2001). This technique has the advantage of using the information about the cases we could find (e.g., district presidential vote, incumbent vote at time t and $t-1$) to make inferences about the cases we do not have. As King et al. note, " ... multiple imputation will normally be better than, and almost always not worse than, listwise deletion" (2001: 51). Thus, while the presence of missing data in a key variable is not ideal, imputing the missing data is an improvement over the alternatives. We have also fit all the models appearing in Chapters 5 and 6 using the other two methods— listwise deletion and assuming all missing cases are non-quality—and the substantive results are similar across all the specifications. That is, there are no variables where statistical or substantive significance hinges on our choice of how to model missing cases.[10]

4.3 Presidential Vote in the Congressional District

In addition to data on candidate political experience, it was necessary to aggregate information on presidential vote share at the congressional district level to determine the extent to which the underlying liberal-conservative sentiment in the district independently impacts the congressional vote. Since presidential vote share at the congressional district level was not compiled prior to the early 1950s, we had to construct such a measure for the elections of interest in the late 1800s and early 1900s based on existing county-level returns. To generate such a measure, we relied on ICPSR Study 8611, which reports both presidential and congressional vote at the county level. Fortunately, our construction of the district-level measure was simplified by the inclusion of a variable in the data set that mapped each county to its corresponding congressional district(s). For those districts composed entirely of whole counties, it was simply a matter of aggregating the county-level data to the district level. For those districts composed of a combination of whole and partial counties, the procedure used to generate district-level data was more complicated.

For multi-district counties, we followed the aggregation method adopted by Ansolabehere, Snyder, and Stewart III (2001, 155), wherein they included "cases where the percentage of the district's population that was contained in whole counties was at least 50 percent" and excluded those that did not meet this criterion.[11] At-large districts were aggregated for the entire state as a whole, and those totals were used for each of the respective at-large districts if more than one was in existence in a given year.

In Figure 4.9, we plot the number of congressional districts with a split presidential outcome (i.e., those districts where a Democrat won the House seat but the Republican presidential candidate carried the district and vice versa) across the election years in our sample. One pattern immediately apparent from the left side of the figure is that the largest spikes occur in midterm election years when the party of the president is most likely to be punished—the "decline" following the initial "surge" that occurred two years earlier during the presidential election (Campbell 1991). At the same time, we do see a non-trivial number of split outcomes occurring in presidential elections years—especially during elections such as 1880, 1892, and 1896 in the late nineteenth century—when the propensity of split-ticket voting was supposed to be relatively low or non-existent. In each of these elections, the number of districts with split outcomes exceeded 60, which is much higher than the conventional wisdom would lead one to believe. The fact that we do observe instances of split congressional-presidential outcomes even prior to the adoption of the secret ballot suggests that a significant number of voters were willing to scratch out or replace names on the party ballot when they thought it was necessary (on this point, see Ware 2002).

After the turn of the century, we begin seeing much greater volatility in districts with split outcomes between the congressional and presidential candidates. During the first half of the twentieth century, the three most notable occurrences of this were in the 1914, 1930, and the 1938 midterm elections. In 1914, the Republicans gained back nearly 60 seats from the Democrats after Woodrow Wilson's election as president two years earlier. In 1930, the Republican incumbents in the House suffered significant losses to the Democrats as a result of the numerous, but failed attempts by President Hoover to respond to the growing economic problems associated with the Great Depression. Eight years later the Republicans managed to make some inroads into the large Democratic majorities in both chambers of Congress after Franklin Roosevelt's failed attempt to purge the Democratic Party of some of its more conservative, Southern members serving in the House. Also of interest from the figure is the number of districts with split

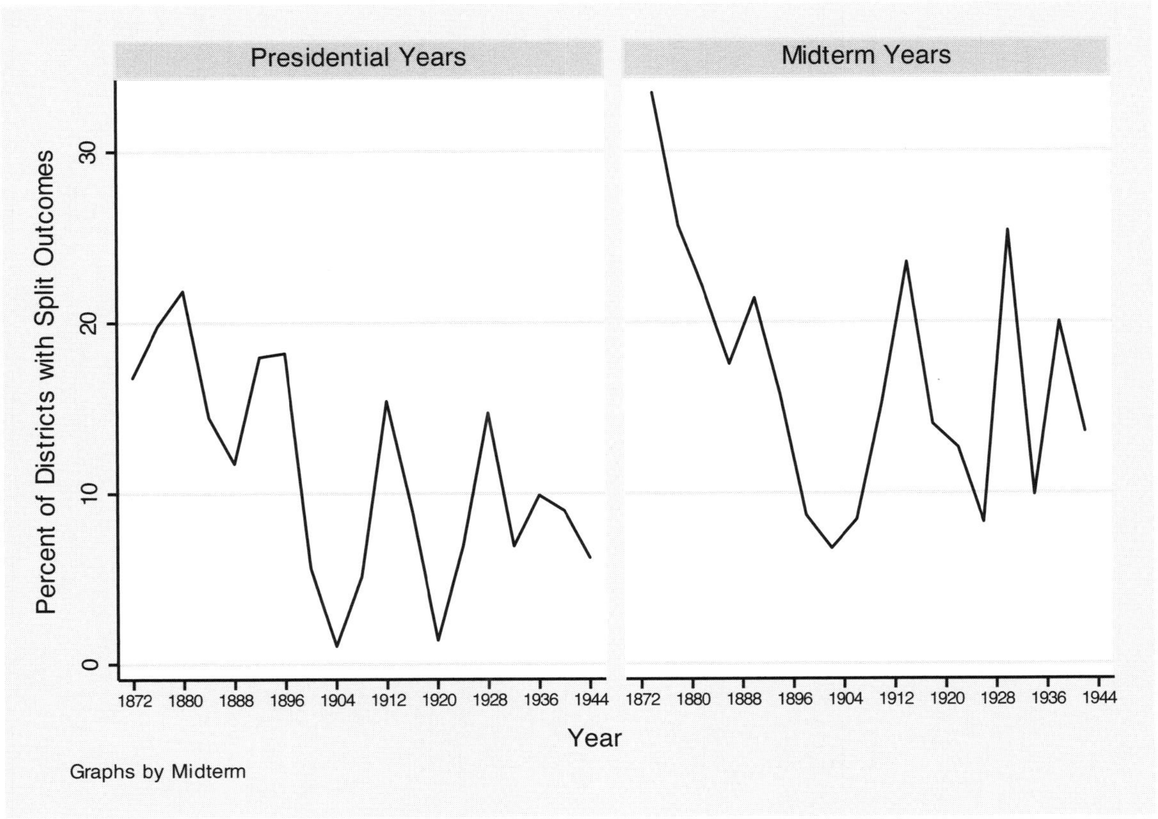

Figure 4.9: Congressional Districts with Split Presidential Outcomes, 1872–1944

outcomes in presidential election years. Despite the adoption of ballot reform near the turn of the century (see the discussion in the next section), we do not observe a dramatic increase in split-ticket voting in the early decades of the twentieth century as one might otherwise expect.[12]

4.4 Australian Ballot and Direct Primary Reform

Throughout most of the nineteenth century, political parties exercised considerable control over the balloting process in the United States. When voters went to the polls on Election Day, they were given "party ballots" that were distributed by the local party organizations rather than printed by the individual states. Each party designed its own ballot, often in a distinctive size and color (and occasionally scent), to ensure that individuals were voting for the party's slate of candidates. Furthermore, voting during this era was not a private act. During the early part of the nineteenth century, most decisions about which candidates to elect were made almost exclusively by voice vote. Beginning in the 1840s, voting occurred by paper ballot in most precincts, but was still performed in the open where the party workers could observe individual voters' choices. This way, the local party organizations could ensure that voters were selecting the "correct" slate of candidates by carefully monitoring the color of the ballots that were selected (Bensel 2004; Rusk 1970; Ware 2002).

As we discussed in Chapter 2, the introduction of the Australian ballot and the direct primary around the turn of the century were two of the most fundamental institutional changes in the history of congressional elections in the United States. In a period of less than three decades, congressional elections were transformed from party-centered and party-controlled to candidate-centered and state-controlled. The fact that these changes happened over a period of years and at different times in different states gives us a wealth of quasi-experimental data that we can leverage to estimate the effects of these changes on patterns of candidate emergence and electoral outcomes over time.

No fewer than five forms of the Australian ballot were adopted in the American states with several states changing the type of ballot more than once. As Figure 4.10 demonstrates, the most basic distinction in ballot type was between the party column ballot, which listed all of each party's candidates for each office in a column on the ballot, and

Figure 4.10: Adoption of the Australian Ballot, 1888–1944

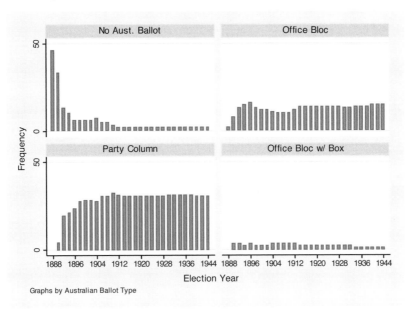

Graphs by Australian Ballot Type

the office bloc ballot, which listed the candidates for each office on the ballot by office. Some states added a "party box" to the top of the party column and/or office block ballots, which allowed a voter to check a box—or later pull a lever—and choose all candidates for one particular party. The final type of ballot was known as a "shoestring ballot" and was a hybrid between the old party ballots and the Australian ballot. The shoestring ballot took on several forms, but was typically printed and distributed by the state. It consisted of narrow strips of paper listing the candidates for each party, plus a blank page that allowed a voter to write in candidates. Voters then chose which strip they would deposit into the ballot box (Ware 2002).

The early Australian ballot laws in Kentucky and Massachusetts were of the office bloc variety, but states quickly began adopting the various combinations described above. Anti-party reformers tended to prefer the office bloc ballot without the party box, as it was considered the least amenable to straight party ticket voting. Political parties adamantly advocated the party column ballot over the office bloc ballot and in all cases preferred the party box option—especially on the office bloc ballot.[13] Data on the type of ballot employed in each state are taken from Albright (1942); Engstrom and Kernell (2005); Ludington (1911).

The direct primary spread much more slowly throughout the country than did Australian ballot reform. The first known direct primary system took hold beginning in 1842 in Crawford County, PA—this type of nomination process, known as the "Crawford County Plan," was employed in numerous rural counties throughout the late nineteenth century (Dallinger 1897). Although the Crawford County Plan was often used synonymously with the direct primary (Ware 2002), there were significant differences between the Crawford County Plan and what most think of today as a direct primary. The Crawford County Plan was put in place by the parties themselves, only applied to Crawford County or other counties that adopted it or some variant of it, and was not regulated by the state. The first modern day direct primary law was enacted in Minnesota in 1899 applying a state controlled, mandatory direct primary to most elective offices in Hennepin County (which includes Minneapolis). This was followed by a law applying the Hennepin County law to the entire state in 1901. Wisconsin took the direct primary a step further in 1903, adopting a law that was much like Minnesota's in form and function, but applying to all elective offices (Ware 2002).

As Figure 4.11 reveals, an avalanche of mandatory direct primary legislation soon followed.[14] By 1910, roughly half of the states had adopted some form of primary to select candidates for office. While the open primary was relatively slow to be adopted, the closed primary took off around 1920 when nearly three-fourths of the states adopted this specific primary structure. Within the span of two additional decades, virtually every state had adopted one or another type of direct primary, which brought to an end the era of party-centered elections where candidates had to rely on party machines or organizations to get on the ballot.[15]

4.5 Congressional Redistricting

At least every ten years, the U.S. Constitution stipulates that a census must be taken, which typically leads to a reapportionment of congressional districts in the House of Representatives. Individual states

Figure 4.11: Adoption of the Direct Primary, 1888–1944

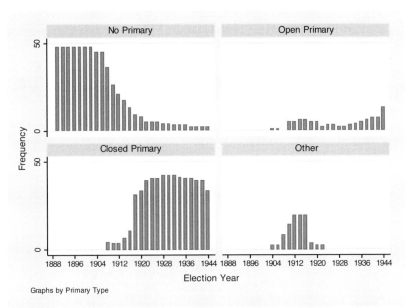

Graphs by Primary Type

may gain, lose, or retain the same number of representatives based on population shifts reflected by the census. During this process (which typically occurs prior to years ending in "2"), every state is guaranteed at least one representative. However, the remaining representatives are allocated based on the current size of the state's population. States that experience population surges during the preceding decade are much more likely to see an increase in the size of their congressional delegation (e.g., California and Florida during the past few decades) at the expense of states with negative population growth (e.g., New York, Illinois, Pennsylvania).

Representative Tom Delay's involvement in the off-cycle redistricting efforts in Texas during 2003 struck many as a blatant and unprecedented partisan maneuver designed only to maximize the number of Republican seats in the U.S. House. Nevertheless, this behavior actually had analogs to an earlier era in American history. Prior to the landmark decisions handed down by the U.S. Supreme Court in the 1960s regarding reapportionment, redistricting within the states was periodic and episodic. Unlike their counterparts in the modern era, partisan legislatures during the late nineteenth and early twentieth centuries had considerable discretion over both the timing and extent of changes stemming from redistricting.[16] Some states went several decades without redrawing congressional district boundaries, while others frequently redrew the boundaries for their House seats, often as a direct result of change in partisan control of the state legislatures. Indeed, during the last few decades of the nineteenth century and first half of the twentieth century, state legislatures routinely engaged in partisan gerrymandering in an attempt to advantage candidates of their party in the upcoming election (Engstrom and Kernell 2005).

Figure 4.12 documents the percentage of states redistricting for each year from 1872–1944. One pattern immediately apparent from the figure is that states did not simply redraw congressional boundaries in years ending in "2" as is common in the contemporary era to reflect population changes during the preceding decade. Instead, states redrew districts as often or as infrequently as they wanted to based on a variety of partisan considerations. Connecticut, for instance, did not alter its district boundaries at all between 1842 and 1912 (Engstrom and Kernell 2005; Martis 1982). Other states opted for more frequent redistricting whenever they thought it might give them a partisan advantage in an upcoming election. As Engstrom (2006) notes, "[I]n Ohio, as partisan control of the state legislature swung back and forth, the state parties redrew the congressional districts seven times between 1878 and 1892, at one point conducting five consecutive congressional elections with a new districting plan."

In addition to states deciding when to redistrict, Congress itself elected not to reapportion congressional districts following the 1920 Census. This occurred for two main reasons. First, there was disagreement at the time over two competing methodologies for how political power should be divided with respect to the distribution of House seats. As such, it took nearly a decade for a method to be settled upon and it was not applied to the states until after the 1930 Census. Second, there was opposition to reapportionment during the 1920s that reflected shifting regional power dynamics. By 1920, a growing proportion of citizens were residing in urban areas, which should have led to more legislators representing these regions. Unfortunately, many rural legislators were reluctant to reallocate seats that would effectively remove existing seats in rural areas. As a result, legislators from rural areas simply blocked legislation that sought to apportion a greater

Figure 4.12: Number of States Redistricting, 1870–1940

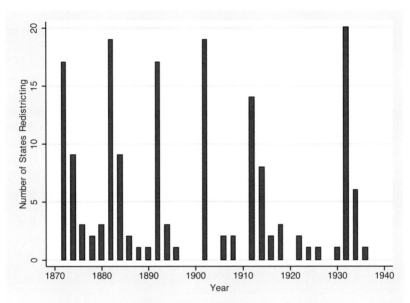

number of seats to urban areas. Moreover, the legislative compromise eventually reached in 1929 did not mention that districts should be comprised of roughly the same number of people. Thus, it would be several more decades before this requirement would be enforced, effectively allowing states to choose not to redistrict if it affected the distribution of rural versus urban seats in Congress.

What insights can redistricting practices give us about elections during this period? One of the consequences of the more frequent redistricting during the late nineteenth and even early twentieth centuries is that it contributed to an increased volatility in House elections during this era. Engstrom and Kernell (2005) demonstrate that frequent redistricting allowed the major parties to "manufacture" competition that would otherwise not exist in House elections during this era. In addition to discussing redistricting practices during the nineteenth century, Engstrom (2006) documents how partisan state legislatures utilized gerrymandered districts to actually determine party control of the House in 1878 and 1888 as well as getting close to winning control in several other election years. Also, Carson et al. (2006) illustrate how redistricting influenced candidate entry decisions during the late nineteenth century, with experienced candidates running in more favorable districts and opting out when boundaries created races that would be more electorally perilous.

To evaluate the effects of redistricting during this period, we utilized a variable which models the extent, and partisan direction, when a district was changed. Because many congressional districts during this era were comprised of one or more whole counties, we were able to use ICPSR Study 8611 and take the two-party congressional vote by county from the most recent election before a new redistricting and then aggregate these votes into the new district lines (Martis 1982). We then took the difference between a district's lagged vote before and after it was modified. This gives us an "exogenous" measure of the extent to which a district was altered, and the extent to which that alteration benefited one of the major parties. This provides a more direct measure of how a district has changed before and after redistricting, which should be a stronger predictor of candidate behavior than simply relying upon a more blunt measure of whether or not each district has been redrawn.[17]

4.6 Discussion

The data we have presented in this chapter illuminate a number of interesting electoral and political trends and provide the framework for the analyses in the next two chapters. Drawing upon the theories of congressional elections presented in the preceding chapter, we now turn our attention to more direct empirical tests in the next two chapters. In particular, we demonstrate that the role played by candidates in congressional elections during the party-centered era of the late nineteenth century prior was more crucial to election outcomes than previously understood. We then demonstrate that the adoption of the Australian ballot and direct primary served to further enhance the importance of individual candidates with respect to both candidate entry and electoral competition.

Next, we demonstrate that the effects of these electoral reforms are associated with the growth of the incumbency advantage over time. Our results strongly suggest that ballot reforms lead to changes in the political market that impacted the propensity of individual candidates to run for elective office. We also evaluate contemporary theories of electoral politics from a historical perspective to illuminate how our results demonstrate that late nineteenth and early twentieth century elections are more similar to those occurring in the modern era than has been previously recognized.

5

The Politics of Candidate Emergence

The stock market crash in October 1929 precipitated the worst economic downturn in the history of the United States. Herbert Hoover, the incumbent Republican president, bore the brunt of the voters' dissatisfaction with the Great Depression in the 1932 presidential election. The Democratic candidate, Franklin D. Roosevelt, soundly defeated Hoover in the 1932 presidential election, carrying 42 of the 48 states and amassing more than 88 percent of the electoral votes at stake. At the same time, control of both congressional chambers shifted from the Republican to the Democratic Party, with the Democrats gaining nearly 100 seats previously controlled by the Republicans in the House of Representatives. Democrats began the 73rd Congress holding more than 70 percent of seats in the House and 60 of the 96 seats in the Senate.

Two years later, President Roosevelt and the Democrats bucked historical trends when the Democratic Party managed to pick up nine additional seats in the House during the 1934 midterm elections. This was the first time the party of the president had picked up House seats in a midterm since immediately following the Civil War. Conditions continued to worsen for the Republican Party in 1936 during Roosevelt's landslide reelection over Republican challenger Alfred Landon. The Democrats managed to shore up legislative control by picking up 12 additional seats in the House. After the electoral dust had settled following the 1936 election, Republicans held a mere 88 of the 435 seats in the House of Representatives, by far their lowest number in decades and barely 20 percent of the seats in the chamber![1]

Although the Democrats looked all but invincible following Roosevelt's second consecutive landslide win in 1936, the 1938 midterm election represented a significant turning point for both the Roosevelt administration and Republican fortunes. In all, the Democrats lost a total of 72 House seats in 1938 to the Republicans, making it one of the worst Democratic party losses at the midterm in history (Martis 1989). Moreover, of the 85 Republican incumbents seeking reelection to the 76th Congress, not a single member was defeated by an opposing candidate. With a 262 to 169 seat margin at the beginning of the 76th Congress, the Democrats comfortably retained majority control of the lower chamber, but with a significantly smaller proportion of seats than was the case in the previous three Congresses. Not surprisingly, some scholars speculated that poor economic conditions such as the recession of 1937 and declining agricultural prices may have cost the Democrats seats in the elections of 1938 (Mayer and Chatterji 1985). Still others attributed the midterm losses to failed policies on the part of President Roosevelt including the ill-fated court-packing plan of 1937 or his unprecedented—and ultimately unsuccessful—efforts to purge the Democratic Party of conservative southern Democrats during the re-nomination stage of their primary campaigns (Caldeira 1987; Milkis 1993).

While the aforementioned factors may have played an indirect role in the sheer number of Democratic losses in 1938, it could also be the case that the Democrats had simply won all the "winnable" seats and had nowhere to go but down with respect to their total number of seats. Such an account is consistent with the work of Oppenheimer, Waterman, and Stimson (1986), who maintain that as the number of seats won by a given party increases over successive electoral cycles, that party becomes "overexposed" and is at greater risk of losing a proportion of those seats in an upcoming midterm election. Implicit in this theoretical framework is the notion that no matter how favorable the national tides are for one party in a given election, there are certain House districts that are essentially not winnable for that party due to the underlying partisanship of the district or the relative safeness of the incumbent.

What all of these explanations lack, however, is an account that explains why *particular* Democrats were defeated while most others were safely reelected. To better understand this distinction as to why certain Democrats lost, we can systematically analyze district-level data from this midterm election. When we do, we see that Democrats endured heavy losses in 1938 as a result of a large number of quality

Republican candidates running against them. More than 85 percent of Democratic incumbents facing an inexperienced challenger won, while only 39 percent of those facing a quality challenger retained their seats. We also found that quality Republican candidates were more likely to run against marginal incumbents, in districts that had traditionally leaned Republican in prior elections, and in open-seat contests where no incumbent was seeking reelection, thus increasing their chances of winning. It seems clear that even in an era that fully predated the emergence of modern candidate-centered elections, we find in 1938 that experienced candidates were adept at both garnering votes and acting strategically when deciding whether to run for elective office.[2]

As the 1938 story demonstrates, candidate emergence is fundamental to our understanding of the dynamics of U.S. House elections. The "passions of the public" that Madison envisioned the House exhibiting cannot be adequately expressed if the public does not have viable choices on election day. There can be no incumbency advantage in House elections if there are no incumbents running. If Republicans had remained demoralized after the 1936 election, they may have remained an insignificant minority in the chamber indefinitely. Instead, by encouraging high quality challengers to emerge, Republicans were able to put themselves back onto the political map. Candidate emergence is the key to competitive elections, which is why we argue it is paramount to analyze the determinants and effects of candidate entry decision as part of our study of U.S. House elections.

The work that most closely mirrors our efforts in this chapter is that of Gary Jacobson and Sam Kernell. In their important study of challenger emergence in congressional elections, Jacobson and Kernell (1983) argue that strategic politicians play a pivotal role in determining the results of both district-level elections and the overall partisan composition of Congress. More specifically, they demonstrate that quality candidates (e.g., those with previous electoral experience) seek elective office when national as well as local conditions favor their candidacy as well as that of their party. As a result, strategic decisions made by congressional candidates, based on factors such as likelihood of victory, value of the seat, and opportunity costs, both reflect and enhance national partisan tides in a given election. National parties demonstrate strategic behavior as well, providing campaign resources such as campaign appearances and contributions to quality candidates running in competitive elections.

Jacobson (1989, 775) revisits his work with Kernell by testing the strategic politicians theory with congressional elections data over a 40-year period from 1946 to 1986. Across this broader time period, he finds that quality candidates are more likely to run when conditions are favorable for their candidacies. For instance, experienced candidates are more likely to emerge when there is an open seat, a weak or marginal incumbent, or national tides are favorable to their candidacy or political party. Moreover, these strategic politicians typically earn a higher percentage of the overall vote share than do political amateurs (those that lack elective experience), even when they run against incumbents. Ultimately, Jacobson (1989) systematically demonstrates that the incumbent's margin of victory in the previous election and the underlying political preferences of the district (typically measured with presidential candidate vote share) are important factors in influencing a potential challenger's decision calculus.

As illustrated in Chapter 4, challengers who have previous electoral experience are far more likely to win elections than those challengers who have never held office. The decision by an incumbent to forgo an additional term in office is another issue of consequence for potential candidates as evidence suggests that experienced or quality candidates are more likely to emerge in open seat contests, thus increasing the level of competitiveness of these races (Banks and Kiewiet 1989; Bianco 1984; Gaddie and Bullock 2000; Jacobson 1989; Wrighton and Squire 1997). Additionally, scholars have also demonstrated experienced candidates are more likely to emerge against an incumbent involved in a political scandal given that their chances of victory are higher against an incumbent viewed as vulnerable or even prone to retire (Groseclose and Krehbiel 1994; Jacobson and Dimock 1994; Peters and Welch 1980; Welch and Hibbing 1997).

What is missing from the literature is a systematic understanding of the dynamics of candidate emergence and of the effects of differences in candidate quality on election outcomes over a much longer period of time. Most of the literature on the post–World War II era asserts, at least implicitly, that modern patterns do not fit elections in earlier decades. To our knowledge, however, these assertions have not been backed up with empirical data. Using the theoretical framework established in Chapter 3 in conjunction with our historical elections data set, this chapter provides the first systematic, empirical analysis of both the factors *affecting* quality candidate emergence and the *effects* of quality candidates on election outcomes in the pre–World War II era. The scope of our data provides the analytical leverage necessary to account for the effects of the emergence of the Australian ballot and the direct primary system of nominating candidates. As we noted in Chapter 3, these two electoral reforms constitute the most fundamental changes to the conduct of congressional elections in American history. Our analysis demonstrates that these progressive era reforms led to a number of unintended consequences including a decline in the overall level of candidate emergence and electoral competitiveness more generally.

5.1 The Politics of Candidate Emergence

Our discussion of the 1938 congressional elections clearly suggests that the relative qualities of congressional candidates could exert a significant influence on House elections occurring prior to World War II. Given the importance of candidate quality on elections in the modern era, we think it is important to explore the dynamics of candidate emergence more systematically across a large number of elections during the late nineteenth and early twentieth centuries. As we discussed in Chapter 3, we believe there are compelling reasons why we might observe non-random patterns of candidate emergence in all time periods, even during the period of party dominance of campaigns. Clearly, the incentives driving entry and exit decisions have changed over the course of history, but our argument is that the different mechanisms were all designed with one end result in mind—winning elections. What changed across this time period is that parties went from trying to win as teams to an era in which candidates now sought to win as individuals. Below we provide the first systematic examination of this evolution to better understand the dynamics of the individual and collective decision making processes.

Based on our earlier theoretical discussion, we expect to see quality candidates emerge in the races that are most winnable for their party. We view "winnability" as a function of factors such as the economy, previous vote in the district, and the quality of the opposing candidate. To begin to systematically test our expectations regarding candidate emergence, we fit the following equation via logistic regression for each of the two major parties separately:

$$Q_{it} = \alpha + \beta_1 DTP_{it-1} + \beta_2 IR_{it} + \beta_3 PD_{it} + \beta_4 MAJ_{it} +$$
$$\sum_t \beta_{5t} Year_t + \sum_j \beta_{6j} State_j + \epsilon_{it} \qquad (5.1)$$

where Q is a dummy variable taking on the value of 1 if the party runs an incumbent or quality candidate, DTP refers to the Democratic percentage of the two-party vote, and IR refers to the presence of an incumbent, which is coded 1 if the opposing party is running an incumbent. PD refers to the party defending the seat, coded 1 if the party is defending the seat, while MAJ is coded 1 if the party holds a congressional majority heading into the election.

The results, presented in Table 5.1, suggest that previous vote in the district and the presence of an incumbent of the out party are important predictors of experienced candidate emergence. Holding values of other variables at their mean, we see that both parties are more likely to see quality candidates emerge in open seats. For Republicans, the probability of an experienced candidate emerging in an open seat is approximately 0.65 regardless of which party is defending the seat. For Democrats, the probability of a quality candidate emerging in a Democratic-held open seat is 0.77, falling to 0.69 for a Republican-held seat. Our data also indicate that incumbents have a strong deterrent effect for experienced candidates. For Democrats, the presence of a Republican incumbent reduces the probability of a quality candidate emerging from 0.69 in an open seat to a mere 0.28. When we examine Republicans, in contrast, we see that the presence of a Democratic incumbent reduces the probability of an challenger emerging from 0.65 to 0.22.

Another key variable that accounts for candidate emergence is prior incumbent vote within the congressional district. As noted above, a Republican quality challenger emerged to face a Democratic incumbent in about 22 percent of races, on average. Yet, this probability varies considerably across previous vote margin—a Democrat winning with a narrow majority of 51 percent could expect to face a quality challenger about 25 percent of the time on average. When the previous vote is 65 percent or higher, however, this percentage drops to less than 15 percent. We find a similar drop-off as the previous vote margin of a Republican incumbent increases—Republicans winning with a narrow majority of 51 percent could expect to see a quality Democrat emerge in about 32 percent of future races, falling to around 18 percent if

Table 5.1: Factors Affecting Quality Challenger Emergence in House Elections, 1872–1944

Variable	Democrats	Republicans
Lagged Democratic Vote	0.03*	−0.04*
	(0.001)	(0.003)
Incumbent Running	−1.70*	−1.88*
	(0.05)	(0.05)
Defending Seat	0.21*	0.05
	(0.05)	(0.05)
Majority Status	0.02	−0.46
	(0.25)	(0.27)
Constant	0.59*	5.47*
	(0.29)	(0.36)
N	12,940	12,940
Log-likelihood	−4,495.83	−3,987.78
$\chi^2_{(86)}$	8,624.65	9,891.79

Note: Estimates are from a logit model with the presence of a quality candidate or incumbent as the dependent variable. Standard errors in parentheses. State and year fixed-effects estimated but not reported. $* = p \leq 0.05$.

they won the previous election with at least 65 percent of the vote. Thus, it seems clear that quality candidates emerged in a strategic and predictable fashion. Just like in the modern era, factors such as the presence of an incumbent, the party defending the seat, and the vote margin in the previous election are all important predictors of candidate emergence for both parties.

5.1.1 The Economy and Candidate Emergence

In the modern era, there is little doubt that U.S. national elections are influenced by changing economic conditions. Indeed, one factor that is thought to play a major role in candidate emergence decisions today is the condition of the economy in the United States. A series of scholars (Alesina and Rosenthal 1989; Erikson 1990; Jacobson 1990; Kramer 1971; Lynch 2002; Stigler 1973) have noted that many Americans use the state of the economy as a device to determine whether or not to support the incumbent party in national elections. Additionally, a central tenet of the strategic politicians theory presented by Jacobson and Kernell (1983) is that the state of the economy in the months leading up to an election has a strong effect on the candidate emergence and retirement patterns. When the economy is strong, majority party incumbents tend to seek reelection in larger numbers and the out party struggles to recruit high quality candidates. In contrast, poor economic conditions tend to increase retirements in the majority party as incumbents en masse suddenly decide that they prefer to "spend more time with their family" rather than seek reelection to avoid the increased risk of losing. In the wake of these retirements, the majority party typically struggles to find quality replacements, while the out party produces a bumper crop of high quality, well-funded challengers who presumably have less interest in spending quality time with their families. Jacobson and Kernell (1983) find little *direct* evidence that the economy affects voting behavior in modern day congressional elections. Rather, voters seemingly respond to the candidate emergence patterns that are shaped by the economy.

Since the work of Jacobson and Kernell (1983) focuses only on post–World War II elections, we know significantly less about the impact of the economy on congressional elections prior to this time. In certain respects, it might appear as though many of the elections during this era would not be directly affected by economic factors given the types of ballots employed and the candidate recruitment system in place prior to the introduction of the direct primary. If one takes a closer look, however, it appears that many of the largest shifts in membership of the House occurred directly following an economic downturn or recession (see, e.g., the elections following the Panic of 1873 or 1893 and the depression resulting from the collapse of the stock market in 1929). In light of the dramatic turnover among House members following each of these periods of economic turmoil in the nation, one is tempted to ask—to what extent should we be looking for evidence of economic effects on congressional elections during the late nineteenth and early twentieth centuries?

Although there is little evidence of individual-level economic effects on House races in the scholarly literature, Lynch (2002) provides a systematic account of the effects of changes in the macro-economy on aggregate House election outcomes over time. He argues that the late nineteenth century saw a substantial increase in the role of Congress in the national economy. Issues such as the tariff and monetary policy dominated the national political discussion as well as congressional agenda. Further, the two parties staked out clear, consistent, but divergent views on these issues, which made it easier for voters to align their personal views with those of candidates and parties. Lynch suggests that prior to the creation of the Federal Reserve in 1913, Congress played the paramount role in setting monetary policy throughout the country, and as a result, voters rewarded and punished the majority party in Congress accordingly—especially in midterm election years. His argument also stipulates that there was a sharp breakpoint in the effects of the economy on congressional elections after the creation of the Federal Reserve in 1913. Given the longitudinal nature of our data, we have a unique opportunity to determine if these aggregate-level effects are also present at the candidate level. Indeed, to assess the independent effect of the economy on candidate emergence at the district level we refit equation 5.1, adding in a variable for the change in the gross national product and interacting this term with whether or not the party in question held a majority going into the congressional election.[3]

The results, presented in Table 5.2, indicate that economic conditions were indeed related to candidate emergence in House elections held before 1913. More specifically, for both parties we see an increased probability of a quality challenger emerging in years with high GNP growth—if the party held a majority of seats in the House of Representatives in a given election year. Substantively, we find that in a year with high economic growth, such as 1880, holding all else equal, the probability of a quality Democratic candidate emerging is approximately 10 percent higher than in a year with slightly negative economic growth, like 1876. This is an especially interesting and important finding in that it demonstrates that economic considerations did play a role in influencing individual-level House races outside of the contemporary era. Thus, just like in the modern era, candidates and parties considered economic factors when deciding which House races to contest in a given election year. Moreover, the findings reported here suggest that candidate emergence patterns are a significant factor in explaining *how* macro-economic conditions affected election outcomes

Table 5.2: Economic Conditions and Quality Challenger Emergence in House Elections, 1872–1912

Variable	Democrats	Republicans
Lagged Democratic Vote	0.02*	−0.03*
	(0.003)	(0.003)
Incumbent Running	−1.34*	−1.58*
	(0.06)	(0.06)
Party Defending Seat	0.19*	0.18*
	(0.06)	(0.06)
Majority Status	0.21*	−0.70*
	(0.07)	(0.08)
Change in GNP	1.03	0.81
	(1.45)	(1.42)
Change in GNP * Maj. Status	4.82*	6.68*
	(2.01)	(2.24)
Constant	0.33	4.55*
	(0.31)	(0.49)
N	6,471	6,471
Log-likelihood	−2,750.23	-2,384.15
$\chi^2_{(49)}$	2,975.94	3,630.81

Note: Estimates are from a logit model with the presence of a quality candidate or incumbent as the dependent variable. Standard errors in parentheses. State and year fixed-effects estimated but not reported. $* = p \leq 0.05$.

in the pre–Federal Reserve era even when controlling for a myriad of other factors.

5.1.2 The Direct Primary and Candidate Emergence

As we noted in Chapter 3, prior to the adoption of the direct primary throughout the U.S., most, if not all, party nominations for individual House races were decided in statewide party conventions. These conventions were largely composed of party officials who were chosen as delegates in a party caucus style meeting. In many respects, these party conventions were high points for party officials, prospective candidates, and voters as all those involved were treated to rousing speeches, party propaganda, and considerable excitement as the party's slate of candidates was selected. With the changes in American society, especially pertaining to shift from an agrarian to a more urban population, the flaws in the caucus-convention system were made apparent. Among the more serious problems were a lack of mass participation in the caucuses, logistical difficulties in conducting caucuses as the country increased in size, and the relative difficulties encountered by the parties in controlling appointed officials (Reynolds 2006). On occasion, these conventions would turn volatile or unpredictable when two or more viable candidates emerged to compete for a particular office. In short, a more effective and efficient means of nominating candidates was needed.

In considering alternatives to the existing nomination system, the answer that immediately became apparent was the direct primary of the "Crawford County" system of nominations. As we discussed in Chapter 3, the direct primary spread rapidly throughout the country. Unfortunately, the party organizations failed to anticipate that the shift to the direct primary would have a number of unintended consequences on their ability to recruit candidates for office as they once did. As voters became involved in selecting candidates to run in congressional races, parties were no longer able to insure consistency in the message and loyalty among candidates bearing their name. Eventually, candidates for House races began running more individualized campaigns in an attempt to appeal more directly to the masses rather than seeking to bolster the party's collective reputation.

The empirical question that we address here is how did the adoption of the direct primary alter candidate emergence patterns? For ambitious and strategic politicians, the incentive structure changed quite dramatically with the movement toward the direct primary. On the one hand, the loss of the party insurance mechanism increased the cost of candidate entry as the candidates themselves had to bear the full risk of running (i.e., they are now insuring themselves). Nevertheless, individuals now controlled their own electoral destiny. In particular, they could decide when to run and what message to convey to the voters. If the risks of entry were perceived to be too high or uncertain, then strategic politicians would now avoid entering races that might result in a loss. Thus, for the individual candidate, the shift to the direct primary was likely beneficial as strategic politicians found it easier to build a long-term career in the office rather than in the party. For the system as a whole, however, the loss of the subsidy on ballot entry reduced the supply of quality candidates in the electoral system. Our data set will allow us to estimate both the magnitude of the subsidy and how it affected the overall political marketplace. To do so, we refit equation 5.1 for elections with and without the direct primary, by party.[4]

The results, presented in Table 5.3, reveal that the same set of strategic factors affects candidate emergence both with and without the direct primary. A Democratic quality challenger is more likely to emerge when the previous election in the district was competitive and in an open seat than against an incumbent with a high previous vote margin. Similarly, the previous Democratic vote percentage in the district and the presence of a Democratic incumbent retard the emergence of Republican quality candidates regardless of whether they have to go through the party or through a direct primary to get onto the ballot.

Yet, when we look at the *magnitude* of these two variables—previous vote in the district and presence of an incumbent—we begin to see how the direct primary fundamentally changed the dynamics of candidate emergence. In open seats defended by the opposing party, we see a high probability of a quality candidate emerging regardless of whether they must go through a primary. For Democrats, holding all else equal, the probability of a quality candidate emerging in an open seat with no direct primary is 0.73, but falls to 0.63 when the candidate must go through a direct primary.[5] The effect is less pronounced for Republicans—without a primary the probability of emergence is 0.67, falling to 0.64 with a direct primary.[6] So the direct primary certainly seems to suppress emergence in open seats, but not consistently across both parties.

Table 5.3: Effect of the Direct Primary on Candidate Emergence in House Elections, 1872–1944

Variable	Democrats		Republicans	
	No Primary	Primary	No Primary	Primary
Lagged Democratic Vote	0.02*	0.04*	−0.03*	−0.05*
	(0.003)	(0.004)	(0.004)	(0.005)
Incumbent Running	−1.41*	−2.15*	−1.61*	−2.38*
	(0.06)	(0.08)	(0.07)	(0.10)
Party Defending Seat	0.21*	−0.11	−0.20*	0.23*
	(0.06)	(0.09)	(0.06)	(0.09)
Majority Status	0.41	−0.49	3.02*	0.53
	(0.94)	(0.79)	(1.26)	(0.95)
Constant	0.45	−1.59	2.08	5.55*
	(0.32)	(1.38)	(1.21)	(1.21)
N	6,526	6,607	6,471	6,153
Log-likelihood	−2,531.34	−1,851.82	−2,258.88	−1,619.47

Note: Estimates are from a logit model with the presence of a quality candidate or incumbent as the dependent variable. Standard errors in parentheses. State and year fixed-effects estimated but not reported.
$* = p \leq 0.05$.

Turning to situations in which a would-be candidate is forced to face off against an opposing party incumbent, we begin to see the political costs associated with the adoption of the direct primary. Holding all else equal, we estimate that the probability of a quality Democrat emerging to face a Republican incumbent in the era before the direct primary was 0.40; however, once the direct primary is adopted by most states, this probability falls to 0.17. The effect is just as pronounced for seats held by Democratic incumbents—with no direct primary we estimate the probability of a quality Republican emerging to be 0.29, but with a direct primary, this estimate again falls by more than 50 percent to a mere 0.14! This is strong and compelling evidence that the direct primary significantly depressed the supply of quality candidates across parties and across election types. The direct primary suppressed the supply of quality candidates seemingly across all levels of previous vote in the district. Figures 5.1 and 5.2 present these effects graphically. In each case, we see the dramatic effect that the direct primary had on candidate emergence across the two parties.[7]

These findings provide strong support for our theoretical arguments described in Chapter 3. Prior to the advent of the direct primary, parties had cartel-like control over the ballot and used it to cajole experienced candidates to be part of the party's ticket. By offering a fallback job or future nomination to potential candidates, parties were able to mitigate much of the risk involved in seeking higher office and hence lower the effective costs of entry. In doing so, parties were able to help foster competition in a large number of marginally competitive seats, much more than would have been the case otherwise. Once the direct primary turned the nomination system over to the political marketplace, entry by experienced candidates plummeted in a systematic manner. With limited levers of control, parties could not even promise a potential candidate that they would win the nomination, much less offer any sort of insurance in the event of a loss. Following the introduction of the direct primary, incumbents of both major parties were less likely to face a quality challenger across all levels of previous vote in the district. Many seats that had been made competitive by the parties' efforts to recruit high quality candidates slipped into a competitive dormancy, as a result of the increased risk of a potentially career ending loss that ambitious politicians faced (Rohde 1979). This set the stage for the widespread growth in the incumbency advantage, a decrease in electoral competition for the U.S. House, and expanded careerism in the House of Representatives. In the next section, we

Figure 5.1: Effect of the Direct Primary on Democratic Quality Emergence

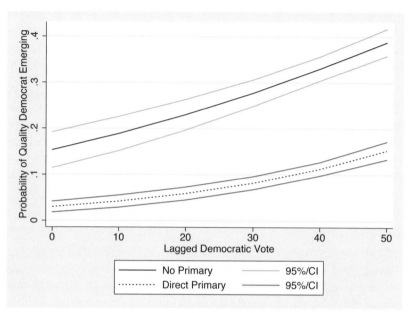

examine the impact of institutional changes and changing candidate entry patterns on election outcomes more directly.

5.2 Candidates, Ballot Type, and Election Outcomes

As we saw in Chapter 4 and noted at the outset of the chapter with respect to 1938, incumbent re-election rates differed dramatically by the type of challenger faced both in the 1872–1944 period that we focus on here and in the post–World War II era examined by Jacobson (1989). For all elections in our historical data set, incumbent reelection rates averaged 61.4 percent when an incumbent faced an experienced challenger. In contrast, incumbents emerged victorious in 92.2 percent of races when they were facing an inexperienced candidate. The same relationship between candidate quality and election outcomes holds for open seat races—an experienced Democrat defeated an amateur Republican in 86.4 percent of open seats, while an experienced Republican

Figure 5.2: Effect of the Direct Primary on Republican Quality Emergence

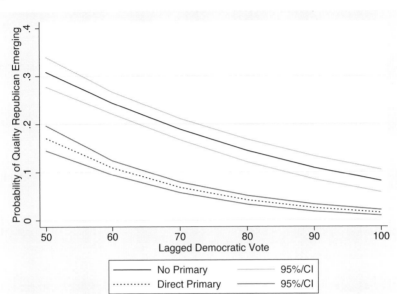

defeated an amateur Democrat in 89.2 percent of these races. When two quality candidates faced off in an open seat, Republicans prevailed in slightly more than than half of these races—53.8 percent. Combining incumbent-held and open seats in Table 5.4, we find that the party with the advantage in candidate quality—an experienced candidate versus an amateur—won 93.7 percent of elections in our data. That is, out of more than 13,000 congressional elections from 1872–1944, we find only 595 instances where an inexperienced candidate defeated an experienced candidate from the other party!

In Figure 5.3 we present these data across all years in our historical elections data set. The data in Figure 5.3 reveal that the effects of candidate quality that are shown in Table 5.4 are quite consistent across time. Even in years in which a particular party takes an electoral drubbing throughout the nation, we still see that having an advantage in candidate quality is strongly associated with electoral victories. The two worst electoral showings for Republicans in our time period were

Table 5.4: Challenger Quality and U.S. House Election Outcomes, 1872–1944

Winning Party	Republican Advantage	No Advantage	Democratic Advantage
Republicans	93.45	54.9	6.03
	(4,051)	(2,162)	(311)
Democrats	6.55	45.1	93.97
	(284)	(1,776)	(4,845)

Note: Cell entries are percentages. Number of cases in parentheses. Uncontested races and races with a major third party candidate excluded.

the 1874 elections, which occurred in the wake of the economic decline associated with the panic of 1873, and the 1932 Democratic landslide that occurred in the midst of the Great Depression. Despite these years being electoral routs for the Democrats, the Republicans still managed to win approximately 75 percent of the races in which they paired a quality candidate or incumbent against an inexperienced Democrat. Similarly, Democrats were routed in the 1894 congressional elections—losing 125 seats—yet they still managed to win 75 percent of the seats in which they held an advantage in candidate quality. They won only 20 percent of races in which neither party had a candidate quality advantage, but managed to win a mere 1.75 percent of races in which Republicans held a candidate quality advantage.

The performance of quality candidates during these electoral landslides provides evidence that advantages in candidate quality can and do provide safe harbor for parties and candidates against national tides. In an electoral system in which individual candidates played little or no role in election outcomes, we would expect to see national tides having a similar effect across all distributions of candidate quality—especially in years with the strongest national tides. Given the massive swings in the distribution of House seats by party throughout the late nineteenth century and during the Great Depression, we are certainly not suggesting that national tides did not play an important role in determining election outcomes. They clearly did. Yet, the simple bivariate statistics presented in Figure 5.3 strongly suggest that the distribution of candidate quality can either dampen or enhance the effects of national tides, much as Jacobson and Kernell (1983) and Jacobson (1989) find in the post–World War II era.

Although the results in Table 5.4 strongly suggest that the relative quality of congressional candidates plays an important role in election outcomes, they are certainly not definitive. Undoubtedly, there are districts that are essentially immune from national tides. Even in today's candidate-centered elections, it is highly unlikely that a Republican candidate could ever win a congressional seat in many of the urban districts in the U.S.; likewise there are many conservative, rural outposts where Democrats are uncompetitive regardless of their relative quality. In such districts, electoral results are often further skewed due to the fact that it is incredibly difficult to convince *any* candidate to take on the out party's banner. However, when parties controlled the ballot for all elections, it was much easier to find candidates to "take one for the team" in districts that were moderately competitive at best.

Figure 5.3: Quality Advantage and Congressional Election Outcomes, 1872–1944

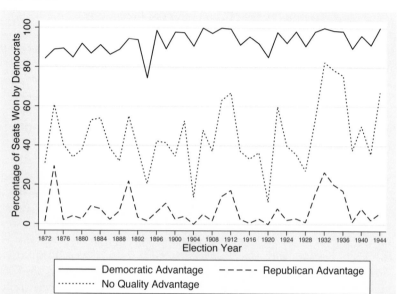

Nevertheless, we would not typically expect to see as many high quality candidates nominated in these districts as we discussed in Chapter 3. As such, it is possible that the results in Table 5.4 and Figure 5.3 are driven by parties and quality candidates simply choosing not to compete in certain congressional districts. This avoidance behavior could produce the bivariate results we see even if candidate quality had no independent effect on electoral outcomes. To get a better handle on this phenomenon we turn to multivariate statistical analyses.

To systematically assess the effect of candidate quality on election outcomes we estimate two models: one OLS model specified as in equation 5.2, and one maximum likelihood model with the same specification as equation 5.2, but with a dichotomized version of the dependent variable taking on a value of 1 when the Democratic candidate won the election.

$$DTP_{it} = \alpha + \beta_1 DTP_{it-1} + \beta_2 DQA_{it} + \beta_3 DQA_{it-1} + \beta_4 I_{it}$$
$$+ \beta_5 P_{it} + \beta_6 P_{it-1} \sum_t \beta_{7t} Year_t + \sum_j \beta_{8j} State_j + \epsilon_{it} \quad (5.2)$$

Where DTP refers to the Democratic percentage of the two-party vote, DQA refers to the Democratic Quality Advantage, coded 1 if a Democratic incumbent or quality candidate ran against an amateur Republican, 0 if a Democratic quality candidate ran against a quality Republican or if two amateurs faced off, and -1 if a Republican incumbent or quality candidate ran against an amateur Democrat. I refers to the presence of an incumbent, coded 1 for a Democratic incumbent, 0 for an open seat, and -1 for a Republican incumbent. P refers to the party defending the seat, coded 1 for Democrat and -1 for Republican. The variables and models borrow heavily from Jacobson (1989) and Cox and Katz (1996) given their emphases on strategic behavior.

The results presented in Table 5.5 suggest that previous vote in the district, the presence of incumbent legislators, and the identity of the party defending the seat all are important predictors of the two-party vote in the district. We discuss incumbents in more detail in Chapter 6, but for now we are most interested in the effects of candidate quality on election outcomes. Our results demonstrate that candidate quality has an independent effect on electoral outcomes that is both statistically and substantively significant over the entire time period of our analysis. On average, the party holding the advantage in candidate quality can expect to receive a 4.64 percent boost in their two-party vote. Given that close to 30 percent of the elections in our historical elections data set were decided by less than 4.5 percent of the vote, candidate quality appears to be an important factor driving election results in this era. Additionally, prior vote share is clearly an important, but far from a deterministic, factor in electoral outcomes. Prior party control also matters in determining electoral winners as the party that previously held the seat is a strong predictor of which candidate is able to compete and win the subsequent election.

Figure 5.4 presents the estimated effect of candidate quality across all 37 election years in our historical elections data. The estimated effect fluctuates from close to 0, to more than 8 percent of the vote across time, but the lowess smoother shows no discernible trend over

Table 5.5: Effect of Candidate Quality on Congressional Elections, 1872–1944

Variable	OLS	Logit
Lagged Democratic Vote	0.42*	0.04*
	(0.01)	(0.003)
Democratic Quality Advantage	4.64*	1.84*
	(0.19)	(0.06)
Lagged Democratic Quality Advantage	1.19*	0.36*
	(0.16)	(0.06)
Incumbent Running	1.37*	0.21*
	(0.20)	(0.06)
Party Defending Seat	−0.98*	0.10
	(0.19)	(0.06)
Lagged Party Defending Seat	0.65*	0.28*
	(0.13)	(0.04)
Constant	26.13*	−3.07*
	(1.02)	(0.34)
N	12,940	12,940
R^2	0.8	
$F_{(89,12850)}$	582.28	
Log-likelihood		−3,321.15

Note: The dependent variable in the OLS model is the Democratic percentage of the two-party vote. The dependent variable in the logit model is coded 1 if the Democratic candidate won and 0 if the Democratic candidate lost. Standard errors in parentheses. State and year fixed-effects estimated but not reported. $* = p \leq 0.05$.

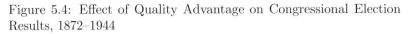

Figure 5.4: Effect of Quality Advantage on Congressional Election
Results, 1872–1944

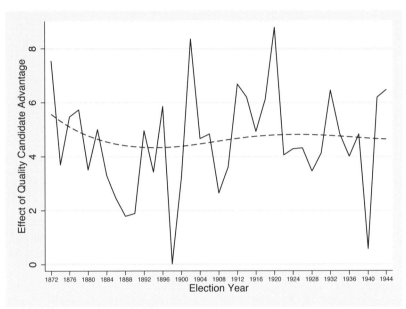

time. It is worth noting that the estimated effect of candidate quality
is always positive and is statistically significant from zero in every year
except 1898 and 1940. We do not have a definitive explanation for the
lack of significant results for these two elections, but they do present
some commonalities. First, both of these elections came immediately
after "disruptive" elections. Democrats lost a large number of seats
in both 1938 and 1896. Second, and perhaps more interestingly, both
of these election years show extremely low levels of both inter-election
vote swing and political risk taking. The correlation between the
Democratic two party vote from 1896 to 1898 is 0.83, the largest such
correlation in the nineteenth century. The correlation from 1938 to
1940 is 0.95, by far the largest such correlation in our data series. If we
examine candidate emergence patterns, we see that the lagged value of
Democratic Quality Advantage predicts values of Democratic Quality
Advantage with a higher degree of accuracy in these two years than
in any other years in our historical election data set. Although we do

not have a definitive explanation for why this pattern emerged in these two years, from a statistical point of view, we see that lagged vote and lagged candidate quality does a remarkably good job of predicting the current vote and is highly collinear with current Democratic Quality Advantage.

The results from the logit model in Table 5.5 largely mirror those from the OLS model, but they do allow us to present the effects of candidate quality on the probability of winning the congressional election. Indeed, we see that the effect of candidate quality on election outcomes is quite pronounced. As demonstrated in Table 5.6, holding all other variables at their mean value, the probability of a Democratic incumbent successfully defending a seat against an inexperienced Republican is 0.92, while the probability of retaining the seat falls to 0.64 against a quality Republican. Similarly, the probability of a Republican incumbent successfully defending a seat against a non-quality Democrat is 0.87, but falls to almost even odds (0.51) against a quality Democrat. These results again demonstrate the powerful effect of differences in candidate quality on election outcomes during this historical period. Contrary to the perceived wisdom concerning congressional elections from this era, candidate quality mattered and had a notable impact on election outcomes.

If we focus exclusively on open seats, the magnitude of the effects on election outcomes is even stronger. A Republican-defended open seat has a 0.84 probability of remaining Republican if the GOP has an advantage in candidate quality, but when both parties have a quality candidate running, the probability of the Republican party retaining the seat falls to 0.46. For Democrats, the probability of maintaining control of an open seat is 0.90 when they have an advantage in candidate quality, but only 0.59 when the two parties each put forth experienced candidates. These results hold across midterms as well as presidential years, before and after the turn of the century, with Democratic as well as Republican majorities, and across all eight decades in our historical elections data. We believe these results *unequivocally* demonstrate that congressional candidates had a major impact on election outcomes prior to the emergence of what is traditionally considered an era of candidate-centered elections. Of all the variables we have used to explain election outcomes during this time period, the candidate quality differential has the largest substantive effect on both the vote share and the party winning the House election.

Table 5.6: Challenger Quality and U.S. House Election Outcomes, 1872–1944

Incumbent Party	Republican Advantage	No Advantage	Democratic Advantage
Republican Incumbent	0.13	0.49	n/a
	(3,568)	(1,307)	(n/a)
Democratic Incumbent	n/a	0.64	0.92
	(n/a)	(1,219)	(4,250)
Open Seat Republican	0.16	0.46	0.88
	(520)	(641)	(204)
Open Seat Democrat	0.18	0.59	0.90
	(151)	(548)	(571)

Note: Cell entries are predicted probability that the Democratic candidate wins. Number of cases in parentheses. Uncontested races and races with a major third party candidate excluded.

5.3 Ballot Reform and Election Outcomes

In the previous section, we demonstrated that relative differences in candidate quality had an immense effect on election outcomes during the 1872–1944 period. Yet these eight decades saw vast changes in how elections were conducted throughout the country. None of these changes was more significant than the switch from party-printed ballots to the Australian ballot. As discussed previously, states rapidly adopted the Australian ballot in place of the party strip ballot in the years surrounding the turn of the century. Moreover, our theoretical expectations are that adoption of the Australian ballot should enhance the effect of congressional candidates on election outcomes at the expense of party influence. The party-printed ballot focused the attention of the voter on the party as it was quite difficult for a voter to cast a split ticket with a party ballot. As as result, we should see more straight-ticket voting and less room for individual candidacies to trump partisan voting behavior (Rusk 1970). The Australian ballot, on the other hand, created a more direct link between the voter and individual candidates, allowing voters to easily choose candidates of more than one party without the risk of retribution from party "henchmen" (Reynolds 2006). As we noted in Chapter 2, many scholars have focused on the effects of the Australian ballot on split-ticket voting—finding considerable evidence that the split-ticket voting increased after the adoption of the secret ballot (Rusk 1970). Our focus here is more election-specific—that is, we are interested in the interaction between ballot type and candidate quality in explaining congressional election outcomes.

Given that the Australian ballot focused the attention of voters on individual candidates, we expect the effects of candidate quality on election outcomes to be enhanced. As candidates began to emphasize personal characteristics more in their campaigns and legislative activities, voters began to focus more on the attributes of individual candidates, which meant that candidate-specific attributes began to more directly affect electoral outcomes. Research to date has suggested that the adoption of the Australian ballot should have led to a greater emphasis on candidate attributes in congressional elections (Engstrom and Kernell 2005; Jacobson 2009; Katz and Sala 1996). In particular, these scholars argue that the personal vote should be stronger after the adoption of the Australian ballot as a result of the decoupling between specific offices listed on the ballot.

In a departure from existing literature, we expect the effects of the Australian ballot to be non-uniform across the different types of ballot employed. Given the battles at the state level over the *type* of ballot employed as we laid out in more detail in Chapter 3, our theoretical expectation is that the office bloc ballot is most likely to prompt voters to focus on individual candidates, while the party column ballot would be more likely to facilitate straight party ticket voting and would be more analogous to the party ballot. As Ware (2002) points out, the major parties typically did not fight the secret ballot; instead, they fought for the party column ballot over the office bloc. Failing that, parties wanted the "party box" on the ballot to help facilitate straight-ticket voting. This was in part because the office bloc ballot made ticket splitting easier, but it was also undeniable that the office bloc ballot effectively disenfranchised many poor, uneducated, and illiterate voters.

As Engstrom and Roberts (2009) note, pitched battles in New York and Maryland centered on the question of what form of the Australian ballot to employ. They note that Democrats in Maryland eventually came to favor the office bloc ballot in part because it would restrict voting among African Americans. Similarly, they note that New York Democrats opposed the office bloc ballot for over a decade out of a fear of losing large numbers of illiterate voters. The evidence suggests that in general, the ruling majority party preferred a ballot structure that encouraged the voter to focus on parties as teams of candidates rather than considering individual candidates for each office (Engstrom and Kernell 2005). As a result, we would expect the effect of candidate quality to differ by ballot type. More specifically, candidate quality should have a larger effect on election outcomes under the office bloc ballot, since this type of ballot gives voters the opportunity to focus more directly on individual candidates running for each of the House races.

To test our expectations regarding the Australian ballot we re-fit equation 5.2 for four subsets of our data: (1) elections taking place under the party ballot; (2) elections taking place under the party column form of the Australian ballot; (3) elections taking place under the office bloc form of the Australian ballot; and (4) elections taking place under the office bloc ballot but with a "box" allowing straight-ticket voting. The results of these models are presented in Table 5.7.[8] The results indicate that previous vote in the district is an important predictor of the current vote regardless of ballot type. This

Table 5.7: Effect of Ballot Type and Candidate Quality on House Elections, 1872–1944

Variable	Party Ballot	Party Column	Office Bloc	OB-Box
Lagged Democratic Vote	0.30*	0.41*	0.40*	0.33*
	(0.02)	(0.02)	(0.02)	(0.04)
Democratic Quality Advantage	3.48*	3.73	6.85	5.66
	(0.27)	(0.26)	(0.46)	(0.85)
Lagged Democratic Quality Advantage	1.68*	1.19*	1.43*	1.89*
	(0.24)	(0.22)	(0.37)	(0.78)
Incumbent Running	1.87*	0.37	0.32	0.64
	(0.26)	(0.33)	(0.53)	(1.20)
Party Defending Seat	−0.56*	−0.35	−0.34	−0.64
	(0.24)	(0.31)	(0.54)	(1.16)
Lagged Party Defending Seat	0.76*	0.42*	0.36	−0.17
	(0.18)	(0.18)	(0.31)	(0.55)
Constant	31.25*	32.79*	37.45*	4.57*
	(1.17)	(1.23)	(2.04)	(0.10)
N	5,407	4,785	3,367	751
R^2	0.76	0.86	0.81	0.59

Note: Estimates are from a series of OLS models with the Democratic percentage of the two-party vote as the dependent variable. Robust standard errors in parentheses. State and year fixed-effects estimated but not reported. $* = \leq 0.05$.

is not particularly surprising and largely consistent with prior evidence. However, the effects of candidate quality across ballot type are much more revealing. First, the effect of a candidate quality differential is almost twice as large under the office bloc ballot as it is under the party ballot. Second, there is no discernible difference in our estimates of the effect of candidate quality between the old party ballot and the party column form of the Australian ballot. Third, the effects of candidate quality under the office bloc ballot are attenuated by the presence of the party box on the ballot.[9]

These results indicate that the widespread adoption of the Australian ballot significantly enhanced the connection between voters and candidates in some states, but not across the board. The most striking findings with regard to the Australian ballot are the vast differences between the party column form and the office bloc form. In many ways, the electoral dynamics under the party column ballot were not appreciably different from those found under the party printed ballot. When voters went to the polls on Election Day, these party column ballots directed their attention to the slate of party candidates, rather than individual candidates as was the case with the office bloc form of the ballot. As such, our results suggest that the strategy of the major parties to fight over the *form* of the secret ballot rather than resisting it entirely was wise. This was especially true given the momentum behind the change in balloting structure that proved to be impossible for the party organizations to ignore. As Ware (2002) points out, the state-printed ballot helped reduce the agency loss for state party leaders, and shifted much of the actual expense of conducting elections from the party to the states. In states with the party column ballot, for example, the majority party got all of the benefits of a state-printed ballot while retaining an institutional structure that encouraged straight-ticket voting.

The office bloc ballot, on the other hand, seems to have focused the attention of the electorate more on the qualities of each congressional candidate on the ballot and less on the party affiliation of the candidates. This decoupling of parties and office reduced the "coattail effect" of presidential elections (Engstrom and Kernell 2005) and most likely set the stage for a substantial growth of "careerism" in the House of Representatives (Brady et al. 1999b). As the incentives for candidates to cultivate a personal vote with their constituents increased, party organizations found it much more difficult to coordinate and win elections as teams. This change would later have profound effects on relative levels of party discipline in the U.S. Congress since representatives elected on these types of ballots would have more incentive to try to appease their constituents, which would occasionally come at the expense of their party organizations.

For states that adopted the party column ballot or even added the party box to the office bloc ballot, the adoption of the Australian ballot largely meant business as usual—candidate quality mattered, but much less so than under the office bloc ballot since individual candidates were not featured as prominently on the former types of ballots. Our results suggest that the states that were early adopters of the now-prevalent office bloc ballot most likely played a significant role in ushering in the modern day candidate-centered campaigns, perhaps even earlier than is now recognized. Indeed, it may be the case that the emergence of candidate-centered elections could have happened decades earlier than is previously believed due to changes in the structure of state ballots (Roberts 2011).

5.4 Ballot Reform and Party Unity

In this section, we briefly consider the relationship between the myriad ballot reforms that took place in the early decades of the twentieth century and the level of party unity voting by House members. A variety of factors may affect the extent to which a House member votes with his or her party, including—but not limited to—the type of legislation being considered, the competitiveness of the district, the leadership roles held within the party, a member's relationship with the party leadership, and the personal, ideological beliefs of the member. Though many of these factors cannot be measured, we do think it is worthwhile to consider the extent to which electoral institutions are related to the level of party voting by individual members.

How might the direct primary and the Australian ballot affect members' overall voting behavior? All else equal, we would expect that legislators elected after the adoption of the Australian ballot may be less likely to vote with their party on controversial issues that may come to a vote. This is largely a function of the secret ballot offering individual representatives more of an opportunity to cultivate their own name brand with their constituents (Mayhew 1974). In contrast, given the difficulty of casting a split ticket under the party ballot used prior to the 1890s, it was much more difficult for voters to punish individual officeholders at the ballot box (Katz and Sala 1996). Under this type of ballot structure, we maintain that representatives would have greater incentive to be concerned about, and to help maintain, the collective reputation of the party since there was less chance they would be singled out by the voters for their legislative behavior.

We think the logic surrounding party unity voting and the direct primary is even more clear. Prior to the adoption of the direct primary, party bosses and political elites could summarily deny a member renomination if they did not find their level of party loyalty to be acceptable (Ware 2002). Members who wanted to retain their seat in the House, for instance, would likely have been more attuned to the wishes of the party organization since defection carried far greater risk of sanctions. In contrast, the direct primary introduced a entirely new process for determining nominations for House elections. In closed primaries, a representative would have to insure that he or she could win a majority of the rank and file party members. In states with an open primary, however, a legislator's nomination could hinge on the voting behavior of independents or those affiliated with another political party—which could lead to more variation in how often legislators voted with their respective parties. As such, we expect that House members from states with an open primary nominating system would have lower levels of party unity than those in closed primary or party controlled nominations, all else equal.

We test our expectations in Table 5.8. The dependent variable is the member's party unity score in a given Congress, regressed on the competitiveness of the seat, the type of ballot used, the form of the primary, and whether or not the member represented a Southern state.[10] We observe that members who come from competitive districts display lower party unity, all else equal. This is not particularly surprising given that seat competitiveness is closely related to the partisan preferences of a given congressional district. Members who represent safe districts likely have a large number of co-partisans in their district and thus experience less cross-pressuring on votes than do members in competitive districts. We also see that members who represent the former Confederate states are more likely to vote with their party. This is likely due to the one-party nature of the South for nearly all years in our data series (Rohde 1991).

We find that both forms of the Australian ballot and the direct primary are associated with reduced party unity voting by House members. The effect of closed primaries as compared to no primary is

Table 5.8: Electoral Reform and Party Unity

Variable	Coefficient
	(Std. Err.)
Competitiveness of Seat	−0.07*
	(0.03)
Competitive * Party Column Ballot	0.001
	(0.03)
Competitive * Office Bloc Ballot	−0.01
	(0.03)
Office Bloc Ballot	−2.53*
	(1.02)
Party Column Ballot	−2.47*
	(0.99)
Open Primary	−3.77*
	(1.00)
Closed Primary	−1.38*
	(0.44)
Southern State	2.69*
	(0.73)
Constant	87.19*
	(0.92)
N	9,381
R^2	0.01
$F_{(8,2584)}$	9.14

Note: Estimates are from an OLS model with the Democratic percentage of the two-party vote as the dependent variable. Standard errors are clustered by member. $* = p \leq 0.05$.

statistically significant, but has a limited substantive effect. The open primary, however, seems to exert a much stronger pull on the voting behavior of individual representatives. A member elected from a state with an open primary has on average almost a 4 percent reduction in party unity, all else equal. This suggests that member behavior is strongly related to the nomination mechanism. Similarly, we find that both the office bloc and the party column ballot have a negative effect on party unity, with both associated with approximately a 2.5 percent decrease in party unity voting.

We also interacted the type of ballot used for the member's election with electoral competitiveness to determine the joint impact of these variables. The interactive terms are jointly significant and fit our expectation. For a hypothetical, non-southern member who won their previous election by 5 percent and who was elected under a party ballot with no primary, the expected party unity is 83.9. For a member with that margin of victory who was nominated by an open primary and elected with an office bloc ballot, the expected party unity is 77.6. Taken as a whole, the results in Table 5.8 suggest that the type of electoral institutions members are elected under is strongly related to member behavior inside the chamber. Moreover, these findings demonstrate that institutional choice has notable electoral consequences, which fit our overall expectations of these specific institutional changes.

5.5 Discussion

This chapter has covered a lot of ground empirically and revealed compelling support for our theoretical arguments discussed in Chapter 3. We have now provided systematic evidence that the relative quality of candidates running in congressional elections had a systematic effect on elections in the pre–World War II era and as far back as the early 1870s. Our findings clearly suggest that many of the claims in the elections literature about congressional candidates during this era are simply incorrect. For instance, we found that the same factors that affect the emergence of experienced candidates in today's candidate-centered elections were operative in this earlier partisan-centered era. Experienced candidates were more likely to run in open seats than against incumbents and the previous competitiveness of the district played a role in entry decisions for individual House races—whether those decisions were made by individual candidates or parties on their behalf. We also found that candidate quality did not simply emerge as an important explanatory variable with respect to election outcomes after World War II. Rather, it was a significant predictor of outcomes in individual House races well before this time.

Additionally, we have provided the first systematic analysis of the effects of the Australian ballot and the direct primary on candidate emergence and election outcomes over time. Our finding that the Australian ballot enhanced the effects of candidates on election outcomes is not in and of itself newsworthy, but the magnitude of that effect across the two major forms of the Australian ballot—the party column and the office bloc—clearly is. Our results suggest that parties were able to yield to the calls for ballot reform without sacrificing the role of party in election outcomes—provided that they were able to get the party column ballot enacted. This proved to be a "win/win" situation for the major parties. They shifted the costs of printing the ballot to the states and ended the "treacherous" practices of local party operatives who did not always provide full support for the party's slate of candidates for elective office. At the same time, this new party column ballot apparently kept the voter's attention focused on the party as a team of candidates rather than a list of individual candidates.

Our analysis of the direct primary reveals that a reform that was designed to provide a more open electoral system had the unintended consequence of gradually reducing the emergence of high quality candidates in House races. Reducing the role of parties in the nomination process raised the cost of "entry" for candidates and our results suggest that candidates responded by sitting out many marginally competitive races. When this result is combined with our findings on the office bloc form of the Australian ballot, we see a series of reforms that were intended to create more open and less "insider" dominated elections actually produced more entrenched politicians. Incumbents operating under an office bloc ballot in a direct primary state could count on voters evaluating them on *their* merits as well as a reduced probability of an experienced challenger, which most likely contributed to higher reelection rates over time (we have more to say about this in the next chapter). Furthermore, these reforms also are associated with discernible declines in levels of party unity as party organizations likely found it more difficult to enforce party loyalty via strong sanctions, or were more willing to grant members "free votes" in order to maximize the probability that they would retain their seat. Overall, then, our results suggest that the Progressive reformers' successes in gaining widespread adoption of the Australian ballot and direct primary were largely pyrrhic victories—the reforms appear to have depressed electoral competition throughout the country and entrenched major party incumbents.

6

The Incumbency Advantage in House Elections

Warren G. Harding won one of the largest popular vote landslides in American history in the 1920 presidential election when he defeated James M. Cox with more than 60 percent of the popular vote. Following on his presidential coattails were 62 new Republicans elected to the House of Representatives, giving the Republicans a margin of 302–131 seats in that chamber. The subsequent election two years later, however, represented one of the largest turnarounds in electoral fortunes at the midterm for an incumbent president and his party. In 1922, Republicans lost 77 seats in the House, which has been attributed to the lingering effects of the 1920–1921 economic recession.

Despite the overwhelming Democratic win in 1922, 72 percent of Republican incumbents who sought reelection were successful. Looking at the electoral patterns from the 1922 midterm election more closely, it seems clear that Republicans may have anticipated that the midterms posed considerable electoral uncertainty. Indeed, fewer than two-thirds of Republican incumbents even sought reelection in 1922. For those Republican incumbents who faced an amateur or inexperienced challenger in the midterm, 91 percent went on to win reelection. In contrast, 64 percent of Republican incumbents who ran against a quality Democratic challenger lost. Even more interesting is that not one quality Republican candidate emerged to face a Democratic incumbent during the midterm election.

The preceding story illustrates some of the myriad complexities involved in determining the extent to which incumbents enjoy an advantage in House elections. We can only speculate as to what the fate of the retiring Republican incumbents would have been in the 1922 midterm election. Some may have won, others likely would have lost, but the data we presented in Chapter 4 suggests that in a normal year, far more Republican incumbents would have sought reelection. A casual look at reelection rates may lead one to conclude that incumbents fare well electorally even if national conditions favor the opposing party. However, the large number of retirements among Republican incumbents combined with strategic entry decisions on the part of Democrats in 1922 suggests that a more nuanced story is needed. The patterns of entry and exit in 1922 demonstrate the opportunities and obstacles inherent in trying to discern the effects of incumbency on election outcomes. Given that slightly more than one-third of Republican incumbents chose not to subject themselves to the judgment of the voters, it is undoubtedly harder to discern the effects of incumbency on election outcomes as many of the retirees likely anticipated a tough election with uncertain prospects for victory.

Additionally, the fact that all Democratic incumbents ran against weak Republican challengers surely inflated the proportion of Democrats who won in 1922 beyond what we would expect to win with a more even distribution of quality candidate emergence. While 1922 is an extreme case of an unfavorable electoral environment for one of the major parties, the measurement intricacies are not unique to this particular election. National conditions, electoral institutions, and individual decisions about entry and exit shape the context for each biennial congressional election. In this chapter we use our historical elections database to provide a comprehensive account of the incumbency advantage from 1872–1944. Our approach does not solve all the measurement issues noted above, but the breadth and depth of our data series do allow us to make inferences about the changing nature of the incumbency advantage over time.

6.1 The Incumbency Advantage in Congress

To date, few issues in American politics have received as much attention and scrutiny as the existence of, and the basis for, the incumbency advantage in congressional elections. Since the first studies appeared in the congressional elections literature recognizing the advantages accruing to incumbents (Erikson 1971; Fiorina 1977; Mayhew 1974), and continuing with more recent, innovative attempts to estimate the extent of that advantage in congressional elections (Ansolabehere,

Snyder, and Stewart III 2000; Cox and Katz 1996, 2002; Garand and Gross 1984; Gelman and King 1990; Stonecash 2008), political scientists have expended considerable effort analyzing the incumbency advantage. Along the way, a variety of possible explanations have been considered to account for the elevated and growing reelection rates of legislators in the modern era. Among some of the more widely accepted explanations for the incumbency advantage are the resources of the congressional office, growth in the costs of waging a successful congressional campaign, and the limited supply of experienced candidates to challenge incumbents.

Why has the incumbency advantage warranted so much attention? Part of the answer seems to be that, at least in the modern era, once a person wins public office, her goal typically becomes staying in office. As stated by Mayhew (1974) in his seminal work on Congress, most incumbents behave as if they are "single-minded seekers of reelection." To accomplish their goals—however noble they may be—they must be continually elected. Incumbency itself is often cited as the key advantage in attaining this goal (Alford and Brady 1989). The consistent ability to gain reelection often leads to the perception that entrenched legislators are "out of touch" with their constituents, beholden to "special interests," and/or corrupted by the Washington culture (i.e., Potomac Fever). The consistently high reelection rates of incumbents have brought these and other issues to the forefront of punditry and scholarly inquiry alike. Yet, despite the vast amount of scholarly literature that analyzes the high reelection rate for incumbents, there is remarkably little consensus as to why incumbents are perennially successful.

We and others view the relationship between incumbents and their constituents as a simple principal-agent relationship. Voters (the principal) get to regularly choose their agent (the House member). To some, high reelection rates for incumbents are indicative of a principal (the electorate) that is largely content with the performance of its agents (elected representatives). To many others, however, the lack of turnover in the U.S. Congress, in the wake of consistently low approval ratings, is *prima facie* evidence that the principal-agent relationship is fundamentally broken. Indeed, this has been a source of widespread concern among pundits and academics who question whether the advantages that accrue to incumbents make it impractical for potential challengers to mount an effective campaign. Without competitive and informative campaigns, incumbents benefit from an information asymmetry; most of their constituents have little idea how or if their elected member is even representing their interests. In fact, Fiorina (1977) suggests that members of Congress can gain a positive reputation with constituents due to their ability to cut through bureaucratic red tape on their behalf. But, as as Fiorina cynically points out, this red tape is created by the very institution—Congress— that citizens turn to for help. Similarly, Fenno (1978) observes that members develop excellent skills as "explainers" of their congressional behavior. Further, members are often left unchecked as they "run for Congress by running against Congress"—claiming that they alone can "clean up Washington." One student of congressional elections summed up the state of affairs in the following statement:

> Elections are supposed to be the means by which the pub-
> lic exercises control over its government. If elections are
> competitive this system works well. People are faced with
> viable options and make their choices. But if the deck is
> somehow stacked so that one candidate is virtually guar-
> anteed victory, then public accountability is undermined.
> (Krasno 1994, 5)

The need for reelection, then, is the linchpin in the principal-agent relationship between legislators and their constituents. If an incumbency advantage reduces the fear or risk of losing the next election, the incentive for legislators to shirk the interests of their constituents will be enhanced.

As we noted above, concerns about representation and democratic accountability have sparked widespread interest among students of congressional elections to investigate why incumbents are so difficult to defeat. Potential explanations vary, but key questions remain unresolved. For instance, is the apparent advantage of incumbency based on the perquisites and other resources of the office (Fiorina 1989)? Do incumbents have better electioneering skills than do their opponents (Jacobson and Kernell 1983)? Are incumbents simply doing an excellent job representing the interests of their constituents? Have institutional changes in the way elections are conducted systematically advantaged incumbents? The weights attached to each of these explanations have direct implications for assessing the health of representation and electoral accountability in the United States. Indeed, if representative democracy is working, then we should be unconcerned about high reelection rates as there is no substantive difference between a constituency choosing the same agent again and again and a patron frequenting his or her favorite restaurant once a week. If, however, there exist a set of factors exogenous to the principal-agent relationship that are producing high reelection rates, we as scholars should point out these factors and advocate for potential institutional reforms. Although the problems inherent in parsing out all these explanations are beyond our means even with our longitudinal data, we do believe the combination of changes in electoral institutions and the extended time series of data allows us to offer new perspectives on this long-standing debate.

6.2 Measuring the Incumbency Advantage

Starting with a flurry of research in the 1970s first examining the apparent advantages of incumbency (Cover 1977; Erikson 1971; Ferejohn 1977; Fiorina 1977; Mayhew 1974), a variety of explanations have been offered to account for the high rates at which incumbent legislators get reelected in the post–World War II era. Initially, the incumbency effect was attributed to a wide range of institutional features such as legislative casework (Fiorina 1977), legislative activism (Johannes and McAdams 1981), advertising (Cover and Brumberg 1982), replacement among members (Alford and Hibbing 1981; Born 1979), and redistricting (Cover 1977; Erikson 1972). Some scholars believe that the advantage can be explained by legislators' personal home styles in their districts (Fenno 1978), rational entry and exit decisions by strategic candidates (Cox and Katz 1996; Jacobson and Kernell 1983; Krasno 1994), a growing "personal" vote (Cain et al. 1987), and a greater emphasis on television appearances in a candidate-centered electoral era (Prior 2007). Still others place greater emphasis on the role of campaign donations and the increasing importance of money in contributing to the incumbency advantage, especially with respect to the increasing costs of House and Senate campaigns (Abramowitz 1991) and on the growing disparity between the fund-raising capabilities of incumbents and challengers (i.e., the "strategic money" thesis as discussed by Jacobson and Kernell 1983).

In their critique of the existing scholarly literature on the incumbency advantage, Gelman and King (1990) rigorously show that some of the most commonly used measures of the incumbency advantage—

such as sophomore surge and retirement slump—produce biased and/or inconsistent estimates of the advantage. As a result, Gelman and King develop a technique that, they argue, corrects for most of the inherent problems in measuring the incumbency advantage, especially those that rely on traditional measures such as the retirement slump or the sophomore surge. Their technique set the stage for some of the more recent and innovative explanations for the incumbency advantage (Cox and Katz 1996, 2002). The works by Cox and Katz provide the most succinct account of the post–World War II incumbency advantage in the literature to date. Unlike other treatments of this subject, Cox and Katz find that the regularity of redistricting that resulted from the Supreme Court decision in *Wesberry v. Sanders* (1964) drove the large 1960s increase in the incumbency advantage. They suggest that the combination of liberal leaning judges and Democratically-controlled state legislatures drew new district boundaries that efficiently spread Democratic voters across congressional districts in a way that maximized the share of seats Democrats could expect to control in the House, while simultaneously creating extremely safe seats for the remaining Republican members.

One additional argument dealing with how to measure the potential advantages accruing to incumbents merits further attention. A recent book by Jeffrey Stonecash makes the stunning claim that much of the apparent growth in the incumbency advantage is actually an illusion. Stonecash (2008) maintains that most of the increase in incumbent vote margins is an artifact of how uncontested elections are treated by analysts. Most scholars have omitted uncontested elections when studying the incumbency advantage, but included elections that are contested, yet not very close. Stonecash (2008) argues that, around the late 1960s, the number of uncontested races declined sharply, to be replaced by races in which the incumbent won handily. This change, he maintains, explains much of the increase in incumbent vote margins over time in contrast to many of the existing explanations popular today.

Stonecash's point about the importance of non-contested seats is well taken; nevertheless, a number of his other arguments are likely to be disputed by students of elections and congressional politics.[1] For example, Stonecash finds fault with scholars using open seat elections as a reference point in determining how large the incumbency advantage is in incumbent held seats, or whether there is such an advantage. Yet we think that the analytical leverage provided by open seats is the key to making accurate empirical inferences about the incumbency advantage. Similarly, his claims about the role of realignment in the growth of the incumbency advantage are undermined by the growing literature that discounts much of the conventional wisdom regarding electoral realignment (Mayhew 2000).

6.3 Estimating the Incumbency Advantage

As the previous section makes clear, the incumbency advantage has proved to be both substantively important to understand and statistically difficult to measure accurately. We do not claim to have solved the measurement problems associated with the incumbency advantage. However, one comparative advantage that we do have is a much larger time series than other analysts have used to study the incumbency advantage. We think that this allows us to find changes in the level of the incumbency advantage over time and across institutions, even if a precise measure of the advantage remains elusive. Our hope is that the evidence we report in the remainder of this chapter will add additional insights regarding the effects of incumbency and spur additional investigations of the underlying causes and consequences of the incumbency advantage.

The Cox and Katz account that we outlined previously suggests incumbents and high quality challengers faced off less often after 1964 than they did in the 1946–1964 period. They attribute this decline in the "collision rate" to the strategic entry and exit decisions of incumbents and high quality challengers, arguing that high quality challengers recognize the difficulty inherent in defeating a sitting incumbent, and therefore wait until she leaves office to seek the seat. Likewise, they argue that incumbents are also forward-thinking, often opting for retirement when their odds of winning reelection are reduced by scandal, poor fund-raising, or the emergence of a high quality challenger to run against them (Carson 2005). Given that high quality challengers are more adept at defeating incumbents than low quality challengers (Jacobson 1987), Cox and Katz (2002, 153) contend that the greater degree of electoral coordination between incumbents and challengers is the primary cause of much—if not all—of the apparent increase in the incumbency advantage after 1964. Their account suggests that explanations of the rise in the incumbency advantage based on resources of office, fund-raising prowess, and the rise of candidate-centered elections are off the mark. Indeed, as Cox and Katz (2002, 138) argue,

> [M]uch of the incumbency advantage, as currently measured, is not a real advantage but rather a statistical artifact generated by strategic entry. If we are correct, the direction of causality is the reverse of that posited as dominant in previous studies: it is the anticipation of (low) vote shares for their parties that drives incumbents out of the race, rather than the presence of incumbents that drives their vote shares up.

How does the Cox and Katz argument hold up if we look to elections occurring before 1946? Our initial answer is: not nearly as well as it does in the modern era. Figure 6.1 displays the percentage of "collisions" between quality challengers and congressional incumbents from 1872–2000.[2] These data suggest that the collision rate between incumbents and quality challengers was actually *lower* between 1900 and 1946 than it was at any time afterward. From 1900 through 1946, the average collision rate was just under 16 percent. It climbed to 20.6 percent between 1946 and 1964 and then hovered at just under 20 percent for the remainder of the time series. Even with the slight decline in collisions that Cox and Katz cite for the post–1964 era, we see that the collision rate was far lower in the 1900–1944 era than it was in the post–World War II era. Thus, the historical data do not support their claim that a post–*Wesberry* decline in face-offs between incumbents and quality challengers is a sufficient condition for the apparent growth in the incumbency advantage over time.

A second pillar in the Cox and Katz argument is that the differences in electoral success rates between quality and non-quality challengers grew in the post–World War II era, which pushed out more endangered incumbents. They correctly suggest that with the advent of the direct primary, parties became less involved in recruiting candidates for office and campaigns became more expensive. As a result, they argue that the vote-getting power of experienced candidates began to outstrip that of amateurs by an increasing margin. Incumbents, they argue, reacted by seeking reelection at a higher rate against non-quality challengers and retiring at a higher rate when facing a high quality candidate. For challengers, the new electoral environment was a double-edged sword. On the one hand, the candidate-centered nature of campaigns focused the attention of voters on the relative merits of each candidate rather

Figure 6.1: "Collision Rate" of Incumbents and Quality Challengers, 1872–2000

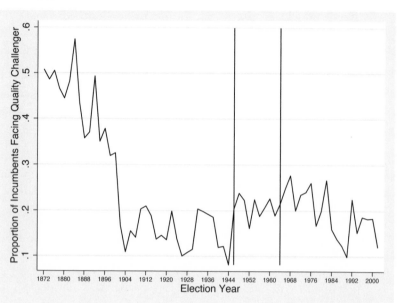

than just their party affiliation as had been the case in the past. To a certain extent, this rendered most incumbents beatable regardless of their party affiliation, but on the other hand the individual opportunity costs of running increased for high quality challengers since losing could mean the end of their political career (Rohde 1979). In a candidate-centered world, more of the costs of vote-getting fall to the individual candidate, which makes challenger entry decisions more dependent on the likelihood of victory.

As we argue in Chapter 3, in contrast to the late nineteenth century, the primary system and the rise in candidate-centered campaigning created a market for candidate entry in the twentieth century. Without the cartel-like control over ballot access that they held during the pre–primary era, parties were less likely to be able to recruit high quality candidates to run in races that figured to be difficult to win. As Cox and Katz (2002, 199) suggest,

> [T]he wave of 1960s redistricting actions led to more isolated

decisions on entry. What we mean by this is that the local parties could less often entice a reasonably good candidate to run against long odds, with the promise of payment elsewhere ... In an increasingly candidate-centered world, more entry decisions were made strictly on the merits of the opportunity at hand and the opportunity costs it would entail for the individual candidate. Thus, the odds of winning the congressional race played a larger role—and voluntary exits by incumbents were more often bad tidings for their party.

Although the Cox and Katz story seems quite compelling if we focus exclusively on the modern era, our initial look at collision rates suggests that the pre–1946 data do not conform to the patterns necessary for the Cox and Katz timeline to be correct. As we saw in Figure 6.1, the collision rate between high quality challengers and incumbents was actually *lower* before the wave of 1960s era redistricting than it was afterward. Much of the Cox and Katz argument is based on the premise that the incumbency advantage is primarily a post–1964 phenomenon. Our historical elections data set gives us the leverage necessary to reassess this argument empirically and cast some doubt on its validity.

To assess the extent to which candidate quality and incumbency may have affected electoral outcomes, we build on each of the approaches developed by Cox and Katz (1996). They break the incumbency advantage into two components: a direct effect attributable to things such as professional staff, franked mail, convenient travel, etc., and an indirect effect resulting from the "quality" advantage held by the incumbent's party and the ability of an incumbent to "scare off" experienced challengers. The incumbency advantage (IA) is the sum of the direct effect (D) and the indirect effect, which is the product of the quality advantage (Q) and the scare off effect (S):

$$IA = D + (Q * S) \tag{6.1}$$

We estimate the incumbency advantage for the 1872–1944 era by employing the two-equation approach used by Cox and Katz. The first equation regresses the Democratic share of the two-party vote in a given district (DTP_{it}) on lagged Democratic vote (DTP_{it-1}), the party of the incumbent candidate at time t and $t-1$ (P_{it}, P_{it-1}), whether or not an incumbent was running (I_{it}), and the Democratic Quality Advantage at time t and $t-1$ (DQA_{it}, DQA_{it-1}). Incumbency (I) is coded -1

for Republican incumbents, 0 for open seats, and +1 for Democratic incumbents. Democratic Quality Advantage (DQA) is coded -1 when the Republican party has a quality advantage (the Republican is either an incumbent or quality challenger and the opponent is neither), 0 if neither party has an advantage (incumbent vs. quality challenger, two quality opponents in an open seat, or two political novices), and +1 when the Democrats have a quality advantage. This gives us the following model, which is estimated via ordinary least squares:

$$DTP_{it} = \alpha + \beta_1 DTP_{it-1} + \beta_2 DQA_{it} + \beta_3 DQA_{it-1} + \beta_4 I_{it} + \beta_5 P_{it}$$
$$+ \beta_6 P_{it-1} \sum_t \beta_{7t} Year_t + \sum_j \beta_{8j} State_j + \epsilon_{it}$$

$$(6.2)$$

where I_{it} is the estimated direct effect of incumbency (D) and DQA_{it} is the estimated quality advantage effect (Q). The results for this model are presented in Table 6.1.

The second equation regresses the Democratic Quality Advantage (DQA_{it}) on the lagged Democratic vote (DTP_{it-1}), lagged Democratic Quality Advantage (DQA_{it-1}) the party of the incumbent candidate at time t and $t-1$ (P_{it}, P_{it-1}), and whether or not an incumbent was running (I_{it}), and is also estimated via ordinary least squares:

$$DQA_{it} = \alpha + \beta_1 DTP_{it-1} + \beta_2 DQA_{it1} + \beta_3 I_{it} + \beta_4 P_{it}$$
$$+ \beta_5 P_{it-1} \sum_t \beta_{6t} Year_t + \sum_j \beta_{7j} State_j + \epsilon_{it} \qquad (6.3)$$

where I_{it} is the estimated "scare off" effect (S) due to an incumbent seeking reelection. The results for this model are presented in Table 6.2.

What do our data suggest about the pre–1946 incumbency advantage? Most importantly, they show that it likely existed in this era. We estimate the direct effect of the incumbency advantage to be 1.39 for the time period 1872–1944, whereas the indirect effect is estimated to be 2.27, for a total incumbency advantage equal to 3.66 percent of the vote on average. We hasten to note that these estimates cover eight decades of elections and hence mask considerable variability over time. Figure 6.2 presents our estimates of the incumbency advantage

Table 6.1: Estimating the "Direct" Effect of Incumbency in U.S. House Elections, 1872–1944

Variable	Coefficient
	(Std. Error)
Lagged Democratic Vote	0.41*
	(0.01)
Democratic Quality Advantage	4.63*
	(0.18)
Lagged Democratic Quality Advantage	1.06*
	(0.18)
Incumbent Running	1.39*
	(0.19)
Lagged Incumbent Running	0.30*
	(0.18)
Party Defending Seat	−0.97*
	(0.18)
Lagged Party Defending Seat	0.54*
	(0.16)
Constant	26.27
	(1.03)
N	12,918
R^2	0.8
$F_{(90,12827)}$	576.74

Note: Estimates are from an OLS model with Democratic two-party vote in the district as the dependent variable. Robust standard errors in parentheses. State and year fixed-effects estimated but not reported. $* = p \leq 0.05$.

Table 6.2: Estimating the "Scare Off" Effect of Incumbency, 1872–1944

Variable	Coefficient
	(Std. Error)
Lagged Democratic Vote	0.01*
	(0.001)
Lagged Democratic Quality Advantage	0.10*
	(0.01)
Incumbent Running	0.49*
	(0.01)
Lagged Incumbent Running	0.03*
	(0.01)
Party Defending Seat	0.05*
	(0.01)
Lagged Party Defending Seat	0.04*
	(0.01)
Constant	−0.32*
	(0.05)
N	12,918
R^2	0.71
$F_{(89,12828)}$	347.02

Note: Estimates are from an OLS model with Democratic Quality Advantage as the dependent variable. Robust standard errors in parentheses. State and year fixed-effects estimated but not reported. * $= p \leq 0.05$.

over time. Our estimates of the incumbency advantage bounce around considerably, but two trends are identifiable: (1) the incumbency advantage is typically *positive* and (2) the magnitude and variation in the incumbency advantage are larger after 1900. These results lead to two related and important conclusions. First, even though political parties certainly played a prominent role in recruiting candidates and conducting elections for much of the time period we analyze, this did not prevent differentials between experienced and non-experienced candidates from affecting electoral outcomes. Second, the growth in the incumbency advantage during the late twentieth century *cannot* be due solely to an increase in the importance of candidate quality as our data demonstrate that candidate quality had a discernible effect throughout the time period covered in our analysis.

To make this point more clear, we break down our estimates of the indirect effect of incumbency into their component parts—the "quality effect" that the incumbent enjoys over an inexperienced challenger and the ability of the incumbent to "scare off" high quality challengers in the out party. Figures 6.3 and 6.4 plot our estimates of these two components of the incumbency advantage along with those found in Cox and Katz (1996) for the period 1872–1990.[3]

Cox and Katz (1996) contend that the growth in the magnitude of the quality and scare off effects post–1964 are the primary culprits in the appearance of the incumbency advantage. The results from our historical elections data set suggest that this is not entirely the case. When we consider the quality effect, Figure 6.3 reveals that it did in fact exhibit growth after 1964, but the data suggest this is a rebound to the level seen in the pre–1946 period and not a new level. If we break the data down into three time periods, 1900–1944, 1946–1964, and 1966–1990, it is actually the 1946–1964 time period that is the outlier. We estimate the average quality effect to be 3.65 from 1900–1944, while Cox and Katz estimate it to be 1.77 from 1946–1964, and 3.99 from 1966–1990. Given that the quality effect was of similar magnitude in the pre–1946 and post–1964 eras, it seems clear to us that the rebound in the magnitude of the quality effect post–1964 cannot be a sufficient condition for the apparent growth in the incumbency advantage.

Figure 6.4 reveals a similar pattern in the "scare off" effect of incumbency. It has clearly been present for the full time series under consideration. From 1900–1944, we estimate the average scare off effect to be 0.54; from 1946–1964, Cox and Katz estimate it to be 0.35, before showing a rebound to 0.49 from 1966 through 1990. Thus, our data

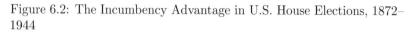

Figure 6.2: The Incumbency Advantage in U.S. House Elections, 1872–
1944

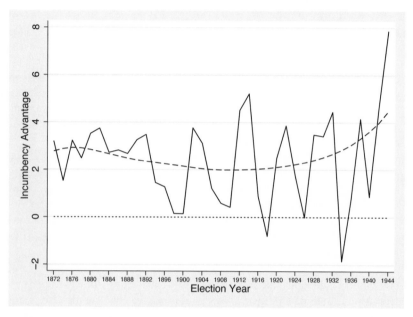

lead us to reevaluate Cox and Katz's conclusions regarding the causes
of the growth in the incumbency advantage. The conditions they cite
as the proximate causes of the growth—an increase in the magnitude of
the quality and "scare off" effects—only hold if we restrict our attention
to elections occurring after 1944. When we extend the time series back
even further, we see that there was a discernible dip in the quality
and "scare off" effects between 1946 and 1964. Our data suggest that
the key question is not the one posed by Cox and Katz (i.e., Why did
the quality effect grow after 1964?). Instead, we should ask why did
the quality and scare off effects decline during the 1946–1964 period?
Unfortunately, while we have sufficient evidence to suggest that the
Cox and Katz interpretation is not necessarily the correct one, it is not
entirely clear what caused the 1946–1964 dip in the effects of quality.[4]

Figure 6.3: Quality Effect of Incumbency, 1872–1990

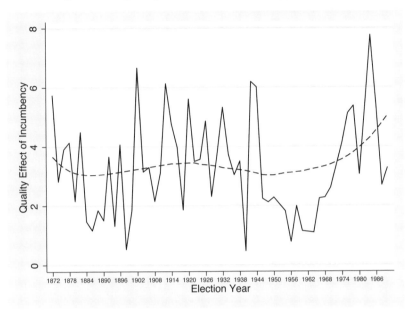

What we do know is that candidate quality has played an important role in entry and exit decisions for a wide swath of history and that making inferences about large time periods from a narrow slice of data can lead to erroneous conclusions.[5]

6.4 Electoral Reform and the Incumbency Advantage

As we demonstrated in Chapter 5, the introduction of the Australian ballot and the direct primary had immense consequences for the dynamics of candidate effects and candidate emergence. We found that the office bloc form of the Australian ballot enhanced the effect of candidate quality and that the presence of the direct primary suppressed the supply of quality candidates running. Given the importance of

Figure 6.4: "Scare Off" Effect of Incumbency, 1872–1990

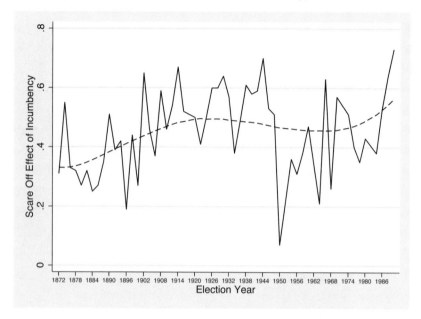

candidate quality and candidate emergence in our estimates of the incumbency advantage, we refit the models reported above for each type of ballot and with and without the direct primary.

The results, summarized in Table 6.3, demonstrate that ballot type and the direct primary do affect our estimates of the incumbency advantage. The smallest estimates of the incumbency advantage are found in states without the direct primary. This is not surprising; the primary reduced the supply of quality candidates willing to challenge incumbents at any given level of previous support in the district. The largest estimated incumbency advantage is in those states that adopted the direct primary along with the office bloc form of the Australian ballot. This institutional arrangement provides a double-barreled enhancement of incumbency: (1) the direct primary makes it less likely

Table 6.3: Ballot Reform and the Incumbency Advantage

	Party Ballot	Party Column	Office Bloc
No Primary	3.29	1.86	3.03
Direct Primary	—	2.52	4.27

Note: Cell entries are estimates of the total incumbency advantage.

that a quality candidate will emerge against an incumbent; and (2) the office bloc ballot tends to enhance the effects of differences in candidate quality. Thus for an incumbent House member, the direct primary is the perfect institutional arrangement—it reduces the threat of a quality opponent and enhances her ability to trounce an inexperienced candidate.

What can the results in Table 6.3 tell us about the trends in the incumbency advantage? In and of themselves, not much. However, Roberts (2011) finds that there was considerable growth in the usage of the office bloc ballot in the post–World War II era. Further, he finds that the effect of ballot type on measures of the incumbency advantage continues unabated; in fact, his results demonstrate that up to 25 percent of the modern era growth in the incumbency advantage can be attributed to the decision of states to switch from the party column to the office bloc ballot.

Another factor that we can speculate about is the direct primary. As we noted in earlier chapters, due to the paucity of open primaries in our data we lump open and closed primaries together. We do think the slight uptick in open primaries that we observe at the end of our data series continued—seven states had open primaries in 1942, increasing to 13 in 1944, and 15 states by 1952. This change could have affected the dynamics of challenger emergence. If the open primary produced inferior candidates, we would expect to see the quality effect dip, thereby reducing the "scare off" effect. If we focus exclusively on 1944, we see some evidence of this; the quality effect is considerably larger in closed primary states than in open primary states. But, without a complete data series, we are not comfortable claiming that the open primary produced any changes in the quality effect.

6.5 The Personal Vote

This chapter has focused primarily on the indirect effects of incumbency, with limited focus on how the incumbent affected elections aside from her ability to avoid stiff competition. While the models presented above provide evidence that the quality of candidates mattered for electoral outcomes, they do not allow us to determine how much quality mattered relative to the incumbent's personal vote. That is, we know that having a quality advantage increased the vote share for a given party, but we do not know how much of this increase was due to the reputation of incumbents (i.e., personal vote) relative to the traits that all experienced candidates brought to a race.

As we noted in Chapter 3, Ansolabehere et al. (2000, 27) uncover "tantalizing evidence of an incumbency advantage during the third party system, pre–1896." They do this by comparing how well an incumbent does in territory they have represented before with territory new to their district brought on by redistricting. The difference in vote share between these two geographic categories, all else equal, serves as a measure of the incumbent's personal vote. They contend that incumbents should do better within the counties of their district that they have represented before since voters are already familiar with them and their policies, which positively shapes their personal vote (Ansolabehere et al. 2000, 18).

In this section, we follow the lead of Ansolabehere et al. (2000), leveraging the regularity of redistricting and the fact that district lines tended to follow county boundaries in order to assess the personal vote accruing to incumbents. Unlike Ansolabehere et al. (2000), however, we are able to assess the effects of candidate quality and the personal vote independently. To do so we reproduce some of our results from Carson, Engstrom, and Roberts (2007) below.[6] In this work we estimate the following equation via ordinary least squares:

$$V_{ijt} = \alpha + \beta_1 I_{jt} + \beta_2 N_{ijt} I_{jt} + \beta_3 (1 - |I_{jt}|) P_{it} + \beta_4 |I_{jt}| P_{it} + \beta_5 N_{ijt} |I_{jt}| P_{it} + \beta_6 Q_{jt}^D + \beta_7 Q_{jt}^R + X_t + \epsilon_{ijt} \tag{6.4}$$

where V_{ijt} is the Democratic vote in county i, district j, and year t; N_{ijt} is a dummy variable indicating whether or not the county is new to the district; I_{jt} is incumbency, coded 1 for a Democratic incumbent, 0 for an open seat, and -1 for a Republican incumbent; P_{it} is a measure of the normal vote in county i in year t, measured as the two-party Democratic presidential vote; Q_{jt}^{D} is a dummy variable for quality of the Democratic candidate; Q_{jt}^{R} is a dummy variable for quality of the Republican candidate; and X_t are year fixed effects. The coefficient on I_{jt} provides an estimate of the total incumbency advantage, while the coefficient on $N_{ijt}I_{jt}$ provides an estimate of the personal vote by measuring the average vote loss for an incumbent in a new county.

Table 6.4: Estimating the Personal Vote, 1872–1900

Variable	Coefficient
Incumbent Running	2.78*
	(0.16)
Personal Vote	−2.49*
	(0.59)
Normal Vote in Open Seats	0.83*
	(0.008)
Normal Vote among Old Voters	0.81*
	(0.008)
Normal Vote between New and Old	−0.02*
	(0.01)
Democratic Quality	4.39*
	(0.25)
Republican Quality	−5.93*
	(0.25)
Constant	18.98*
	(0.63)
N	27,815
R^2	0.56

Note: Estimates are from an OLS model with Democratic two-party vote in the county as the dependent variable. Robust standard errors in parentheses. Year fixed-effects estimated but not reported. $* = p \leq 0.05$.

The results in Table 6.4 cast considerable doubt on the results reported by Ansolabehere et al. (2000) and reinforce our findings that candidate quality played a large role in election outcomes for this era. When the Republican Party chose to field an experienced candidate, the Democratic vote declined by an average of almost 6 percent. At the same time, a Democratic quality candidate increased that party's average vote share across all the elections in our sample by slightly more than 4 percent. Additionally, and similar to the results reported by Ansolabehere, Snyder, and Stewart (2000), we find support for a modest personal vote during the latter part of the nineteenth century. On average, an incumbent running during the 1872–1900 era had an advantage of 2.78 percent of the vote. Given the size of the personal vote coefficient (2.49 percent) in our model, it appears as though nearly all of the incumbency advantage can be attributed to the personal vote of individual candidates. Since most incumbents during this era did not possess the types of resources that are more common during the contemporary era (e.g., large staffs, offices throughout the congressional district), it is likely that most of this personal vote was a function of local recognition of individual candidates.

In conjunction with our earlier findings in this chapter, these results offer several new insights about late nineteenth century House elections and raise important implications about the growth in the incumbency advantage across time. Contrary to much of the conventional wisdom about this era, we find evidence that quality House candidates significantly enhanced the attractiveness of the party ballot, and that parties responded by actively recruiting high quality candidates to run in competitive races. Moreover, the effects of candidate quality appear to have affected the entry decisions of other congressional candidates. Overall, then, our findings suggest that Cox and Katz's assertion that a growth in the quality and scare off effects is largely responsible for the growth in the incumbency advantage is incomplete as a broader theoretical statement. Whereas it may be accurate for the post–World War II era, it clearly does not fit with electoral patterns prior to this time.

Based on the findings reported in this chapter, congressional candidates during the late nineteenth century benefited from a quality advantage and strategically coordinated their entry decisions. Yet, at the same time, the prospects for individual candidates to win a series of elections were tenuous at best as parties often were able to entice high quality candidates to oppose them. For example, we estimate that incumbency provided a 5 percent vote boost in 1882, and over 80 percent of incumbents won. However, in 1874, the advantages of incumbency were around 3 percent, and over 35 percent of the incumbents who sought reelection went on to lose.

6.6 Discussion

This chapter has tackled an issue—the incumbency advantage—that has been analyzed extensively by a variety of scholars in the congressional elections literature. Nevertheless, we believe the preceding analyses have added significantly to this important scholarly debate. We have systematically tested the generalizability of arguments made by Cox and Katz (1996, 2002) and Ansolabehere et al. (2000) concerning the incumbency advantage across the eight decades in our historical elections data set. While Cox and Katz argue that a growth in the "quality effect" contributed to the growing incumbency advantage in the post–World II era, we find a similar quality effect existed throughout much of the history of the country. Our results also raise an important caveat regarding one of the central conclusions reached by Ansolabehere et al. (2000) in their analysis of the incumbency advantage since the early 1900s. Based on their findings, they claim that a large portion of the incumbency advantage is a result of a personal vote as opposed to challenger quality. When we include data on candidate quality in their original specification, however, we find a different result. Although there continues to be evidence of a small personal vote across the entire 1872–1944 era, we actually find that challenger quality exerts a much larger effect on the incumbency advantage than was previously believed.

The findings reported here have three notable implications. First, they suggest that the conclusion reached by Cox and Katz that the quality effect is a sufficient explanation for the growth in the incumbency advantage during the contemporary era is not supported by our historical data. For their results to truly be generalizable, we should have found little or no evidence of a quality effect during this era when the incumbency advantage was much smaller than today. However, we found just the opposite—a robust quality effect long before scholars were concerned about incumbent reelection rates. Second, the results in this chapter once again highlight the crucial role that candidate quality has played in affecting electoral outcomes in both candidate-centered and party-centered eras. While the findings reported in this chapter cannot speak to this issue definitively, our results suggest that both candidate quality and ballot type affected the extent to which voters use party as "cue" in voting. Finally, our results demonstrate that institutions such as the direct primary and the office bloc ballot are an important piece of the puzzle in understanding the advantages that accrue to incumbents in congressional elections regardless of the era under examination.

These results raise provocative questions for future research examining the incumbency advantage, competition in elections, and the effects of candidate quality on election outcomes in congressional races. Most notably, they suggest that reformers concerned with high incumbent reelection rates should consider advocating reforms that would provide incentives for more high quality candidates to emerge. Our results indicate that the current political marketplace simply does not support high levels of political competition in House elections. Reforms that either effectively reduce the costs of entry to the political marketplace or stimulate voters to consider parties as "teams" would appear to have the best chance of increasing political competition in incumbent-held seats. We certainly recognize that these potential reforms could have other desultory effects, but if one wants to increase the competitiveness of House races our results suggest several places to start the conversation.

7

Conclusions

On November 3, 2010, the day after the historic midterm elections, President Obama described the electoral results as a "shellacking" and took responsibility for the significant Democratic losses. In total, 52 Democratic incumbents were defeated in the U.S. House, making it the worst loss for a party at the midterm since 1938. In the wake of the overwhelming defeat for Democrats, some pundits posited that the results were a clear referendum on the Obama administration. After four years of serving in the minority, the Republicans managed to win back control of the House with a comfortable 242–193 seat margin and fell just four seats shy of retaking control of the Senate. With presidential approval hovering slightly below 50 percent, a still sluggish economy throughout President Obama's first two years in office, and a number of controversial roll call votes taken during the 111th Congress, the voters seemingly sent a strong message of discontent to the president through the only means necessary at the time—by punishing members of his party in Congress during the 2010 midterm elections.

One of the main ways the Republicans were able to translate public discontent into a large seat gain in 2010 stemmed from the significant electoral advantage they had in candidate recruitment that year. Whereas one party or the other often has a small net advantage in recruiting experienced candidates to run in a given election year, 2010 was truly historic for the Republicans. For the first time in over six decades, the Republicans had a significant advantage in quality candidate recruitment over the Democrats, netting 32 more experienced candidates on the ballot. Additionally, they were also generally more successful at recruiting Republican candidates across the board. Indeed, in 430 of the 435 House races held in 2010, Republicans fielded a candidate on the ballot, which is unprecedented in the modern era of reduced electoral competition. The combination of the weak economy, an unpopular president, and strong anti-Democratic national tides led to an electoral scenario that was clearly stacked in favor of the Republicans (Carson and Pettigrew 2011).

Just four years earlier, during the 2006 midterm elections, the Democratic Party managed to pick up enough seats in the House and Senate to recapture control of both chambers of Congress for the first time since 1994. The growing unpopularity of the war in Iraq, President George W. Bush's relatively low approval ratings, and the numerous scandals plaguing Republican Party legislators were some of the factors that contributed to the reversal of fortune during the election. Democrats were poised to take advantage of these and other problems that the Republican majority had to contend with by recruiting and fielding a sizable number of quality challengers to compete in open seats and against marginal incumbents. Indeed, many of the Democratic candidates that defeated Republican incumbents or won control of open seats in the election had previous experience in elective office (i.e., they were "quality" candidates) (Jacobson 2008). Thus, it was the combination of both individual and national-level factors during the election that assisted the Democrats in wresting majority control of Congress away from the Republicans.

When the Republicans captured a majority of both chambers 12 years earlier during the 1994 midterm elections, their victory ended 40 years of Democratic control of the House.[1] Due in part to an increased number of retirements among Democratic incumbents in 1992, the Republicans began to slowly make inroads into the Democratic majority in Congress. Two years later in 1994, the Republicans were successful in capturing control of both chambers of Congress in this watershed election as a result of the larger than average number of experienced Republican candidates running for office and the sizable number of open seats vacated by retiring Democratic incumbents. Once again, the relatively large number of quality candidates running in the 1994 midterms and a pro-GOP national tide resulted in a dramatic change in the composition of the U.S. House (Jacobson 1996).

With the exception of these three notable elections, we have to go back as far as the 1954 election to find a shift in partisan control of the House of Representatives. In the decades preceding World War II, however, there were numerous instances of majority control shifting back and forth between Democrats and Republicans every few election cycles. In the 37 separate elections held between 1872 and 1946, for instance, the major parties exchanged control of the House chamber a total of 10 times. Moreover, the number of seats that changed hands between the parties in some of the more volatile election years during this period was quite dramatic at times. In 1874 and 1890, for example, the Republicans lost a total of 96 and 93 seats respectively. Four years later in 1894, the Democrats suffered one of the biggest electoral losses in history when their party lost control of 125 seats in the House. Nearly forty years later, the Republicans would experience a similar fate at the polls by way of a 100-seat loss during the landslide victory for Franklin Roosevelt and the Democratic Party in the 1932 elections (Martis 1989).

7.1 Lessons from the Past

What factors contributed to the greater volatility in elections to the U.S. House during this period? As we illustrated in our discussion of the 1874 election at the outset of the book, many of the same factors affecting contemporary elections were relevant in understanding nineteenth or early twentieth century elections. On one level, this is a bit surprising as many of the historical accounts of elections from this era offer a starkly different perspective. For instance, most descriptions have stressed the volatility that was occurring in these elections, but much of the volatility in individual election years has been attributed to changing national and partisan tides or a general backlash against the party in power as a result of unfavorable economic, military, or policy decisions. To a certain extent, the conventional portrait of nineteenth and early twentieth century congressional elections emphasized their lack of importance in contrast to the candidates who were at the top of the ticket. Macro-level factors such as the predominance of presidential elections, the use of the party ballot, and the lack of voter information about individual candidates running for office supposedly combined to suppress the relative salience of congressional elections.

Until recently, little systematic attention had been given to congressional elections in the late nineteenth or early twentieth centuries. Because the parties directly controlled nominations, mobilized voters, and decided the format of the ballot for much of this era, one might assume that there was little room left for candidates to exert an independent influence on voter behavior at the polls. Even after the adoption of the Australian ballot near the end of the nineteenth century and the emergence of the direct primary during the early part of the twentieth century, most observers did not come to fully appreciate the role of individual candidates in congressional elections until well after World War II. It was only then that political scientists began acknowledging that elections had become more "candidate-centered," with greater emphasis placed on individual-level factors that were contributing to electoral success (Jacobson and Kernell 1983; Mayhew 1974).

Beyond knowing little about elections from this period, we found that a more detailed examination of electoral patterns and trends over time was useful to illuminate a variety of puzzles from the contemporary era. For instance, the decline in competitiveness in congressional races and the growth in the incumbency advantage during the past few decades are two such issues that merit additional attention. As we emphasized in Chapter 1, we believe that the collection of data across time and the comparative advantage that comes from leveraging history have enormous benefits for scholars who are interested in building and testing more dynamic theories of politics. In particular, the greater institutional variation in congressional elections from this period could play a key role in helping us speak to many of the yet unaddressed questions about electoral competitiveness in Congress.

Over the course of several years, we have collected data on over 70 years of congressional elections from 1872–1944 in an attempt to gain a more comprehensive understanding of elections during this era. Through a thorough analysis of elections from this period, we conclude that candidate quality is the most important and fundamental piece of the larger puzzle in understanding the politics of congressional elections across time. Congressional elections during the late nineteenth century, for instance, were much more competitive than those after the turn of the century due to the greater number of experienced candidates on the ballot. While we often think of the late nineteenth century as one of strong party organizations largely manipulating the electoral machinery, parties clearly had an incentive to recruit quality candidates and coordinate entry decisions since doing so maximized their potential for victory. As such, both the candidates running for office and the parties that supported them politically benefited from having a quality advantage when voters went to the polls.

How exactly did quality candidates enhance the electoral fortunes of the political parties during this era? As discussed in Chapter 3, we believe the answer lies in conceptualizing parties in the nineteenth century as teams. In their attempt to produce a collective good in the form of a party ballot, the party organizations sought to maximize the aggregate number of experienced candidates appearing on the ballot in a given election year since doing so would help them attract voters who responded to more than simply party labels. Nevertheless, they recognized that quality candidates were sometimes reluctant to run when local or national conditions were not especially favorable given the risk of defeat. As such, parties came up with the creative solution of offering candidates "insurance" in the form of patronage jobs or promises of future opportunities to run for elective office in the event they lost (Brady et al. 1999a). This party subsidy eliminated many of the barriers to otherwise risk-averse candidates as the potential costs for running and losing were partially underwritten by the party organizations.

To a considerable extent, then, the strong party organizations in control of this process were able to manufacture higher levels of competition in congressional races than we regularly observe today. During this era, parties used their cartel-like control over the electoral system to coordinate entry decisions of candidates as well as entice experienced candidates to run, thus increasing both the level of competition and volatility in nineteenth century elections. With the adoption of progressive reforms at the turn of the century, such as the Australian ballot and direct primary legislation, party organizations began losing influence over congressional candidates. Without direct control over nominations, parties were no longer able to provide the side payments necessary to compel otherwise reluctant candidates to seek elected office. The cartel-like system of party control in place during much of the nineteenth century gradually began to give way to a political marketplace that is more common in today's largely candidate-centered electoral environment.

Given the obvious impact of the changes, why did the major parties not do more to stop these reform efforts? As Ware (2002) and Reynolds (2006) argue, party organizations were not the victims of anti-party reforms that sought to undermine their autonomy and effectiveness in the electoral arena. The major parties acquiesced to the electoral changes given that they did not have nearly as much control over election outcomes as many believed. By the late nineteenth century, parties were losing their grip on voters and some party actors engaged in treachery at the ballot box, which directly affected the party's ability to regulate nominations to Congress. Not only did widespread adoption of the Australian ballot help to stabilize the electoral process for parties by reducing the likelihood of agency loss, it also shifted the considerable cost of preparing and printing ballots from the party to the state and local government, freeing up more party funds for the mobilization of voters.

Instead of objecting to the inevitable reform, parties quickly chose to try to control the type of Australian ballot that was adopted (Ware 2002). In particular, the party organizations strongly favored the party column ballot over the office bloc ballot. Based on our results in Chapter 5, this was a wise and effective strategy. The office bloc form of the ballot appears to have focused voters' attention more on the qualities of individual candidates and less on their party affiliation. As a result, the effects of candidate quality were significantly enhanced. Over time, the use of this type of ballot weakened the coattail effect in presidential elections, established the conditions necessary for the growth of careerism in the U.S. House, and created incentives for legislators to develop a personal vote with their constituents. These changes, in effect, made parties less able to win as teams. However, for states that adopted the party column ballot or even added the party box to the office bloc ballot, the adoption of the Australian ballot largely meant business as usual—at least in the short term. The quality of individual candidates still had an effect, but less so than under the office bloc ballot.

The evolution in party control over the ballot is also useful for helping us understand the growth in the incumbency advantage in Congress across time as we discuss in Chapter 6. When the parties actively recruited experienced candidates to run during the late nineteenth century, this led to greater competitiveness in House elections with neither party able to develop a comparative advantage by way of electoral outcomes. The opportunities for individual candidates to win repeatedly were diminished as both parties were regularly able to entice high quality candidates to oppose them. Over time, the former cartel system of nominations was replaced with a political marketplace, where individual candidates had to evaluate whether running for office was worth the potential risks should they run and ultimately lose the election. With the parties no longer subsidizing candidate entry, the supply of quality candidates in marginally competitive and noncompetitive races rapidly began to decrease. As a result, congressional elections became less competitive, with risk-averse candidates no longer willing to run if a political defeat meant the end of their political careers.

7.2 The Unintended Consequences of Electoral Reform

What effect have the electoral and institutional changes described in the preceding chapters had on our democratic and political system? As is often the case with elections themselves, the long-term political effects have been quite profound. Indeed, and from a normative perspective, many of the changes that occurred during the late nineteenth and early twentieth centuries have had an enormous impact on both democratic accountability and representation in the United States. For instance, institutionalization of the ballot structure during the late nineteenth century and the gradual emergence of the primary system made it significantly more difficult for third party candidates to emerge in congressional races. Not only did the electoral reforms make it harder for third party candidates to gain ballot access, but they also offered the major party organizations greater opportunities to co-opt the positions of minor parties. As the two major parties began regularly adopting issues that were once held by these minor parties, the third parties' electoral appeal began to weaken among the electorate (Hirano 2008).

In addition to their effects on third parties, the electoral reforms also produced a number of changes within the House chamber. Many of the prominent features of the contemporary U.S. House (i.e., the seniority system, property rights on committees, and the party leadership structure) are directly a function of the underlying electoral reforms. With fewer third party candidates emerging than was once the case, and a strong two-party system taking hold in the early part of the twentieth century, levels of electoral competition continued to steadily decline. This decline in competition stifled turnover in Congress, which had the noticeable consequence of increasing the length of the congressional career (Polsby 1968). As legislators began serving longer periods of time in Congress, they starting devising institutions that would allow them to establish their own "turf" on legislative committees and work their way up the hierarchy of the party leadership structure. Within a very short period of time, the framework for the modern committee and party system had emerged in Congress.

As discussed in Chapter 5, adoption of the Australian ballot and primary reform also changed the incentive structure for members of

Congress, who began to focus greater attention on getting reelected. For example, the electoral reforms significantly increased the demands for constituency service in Congress, which led to a steady increase in the number of congressional staff throughout the twentieth century. Over time, members began taking on more casework and engaging in the types of activities that they believed would help them get reelected. Based on the type of ballot adopted across states, legislators also began to differ in their levels of party unity. In those states with an office bloc ballot that placed a greater emphasis on candidate-specific attributes, representatives were far less supportive of their party compared to those members who were elected in states utilizing party column ballots. This, in turn, had notable consequences for agenda control in the House, especially in connection with the majority's ability to achieve favorable legislative outcomes (Cox and McCubbins 2005).

At first glance, it might appear that increased longevity and greater responsiveness among incumbents serving in Congress are beneficial for the electorate. After all, tenure in office could potentially translate into increased levels of expertise when it comes to the public policy process. Unfortunately, high incumbency reelection rates and the trend toward "career" politicians have raised a host of concerns about representation and electoral accountability in Congress as well. Indeed, incumbents who have little reason to fear that they will lose in an upcoming election have reduced incentives to be responsive to their constituents. Thus, although the balloting and primary reforms of the late nineteenth and early twentieth centuries sought to mitigate the negative influences of party machines in congressional elections, one of the unintended consequences of these changes is that it became substantially more risky for strong candidates to challenge incumbents. As such, incumbents today are much safer than they were in the distant past, which means they can actually be less responsive to constituents than they once were.

7.3 Summary and Implications

Taken as a whole, our analysis demonstrates that congressional elections from 1872–1944 look a lot more like elections during the contemporary era than most scholars have previously acknowledged. Experienced or quality candidates did significantly better at the polls during this era than political amateurs running for office. Nevertheless, incumbents seeking reelection during much of this period were not nearly as successful as those in the modern era. As our analysis in Chapter 6 revealed, this is largely because the opposition parties were more successful at recruiting experienced candidates to challenge incumbents, leading to increased electoral competition. With cartel-like control over access to the ballot, parties were much more successful at manufacturing competition in congressional races. With the adoption of the Australian ballot and the emergence of the direct primary, this gradually began to change as candidates became much more selective about when they chose to run given the obvious risks associated with entry decisions. In the modern context, for instance, incumbents have become quite adept at scaring off strong opponents through established legislative records and their fund-raising prowess (Jacobson 2009).

Our own investigation of congressional elections from this period has recast much of the conventional wisdom about these elections. We have systematically shown that experienced candidates during this period were affected by the likelihood of victory and the value of the seat much as they are in the contemporary era. Even when entry decisions were coordinated by the party organizations, politicians and the parties that nominated them exhibited strategic behavior. Candidates may have had to initially seek the nomination from the parties directly, but this did not stop them from doing so. As such, there is no reason to suspect that individual political ambition was tempered by the party ballot. While the adoption of the Australian ballot made it easier for incumbents to cultivate a "personal vote" with their constituents, the voters were not ignored prior to this development. Evidence of an "electoral connection" is present even before this electoral reform, which suggests that voters paid attention and absorbed what was at stake in congressional elections from this era.

One of the consequences of greater control by the parties during the late nineteenth century was increased electoral competition. However, this competition came at a relatively high cost—greater electoral corruption in the form of coercive and fraudulent election practices emanating from the "smoke-filled" nominating caucuses (Bensel 2004; Summers 2004). By the early twentieth century, the widespread adoption of progressive reform legislation in the form of secret ballot laws and direct primaries seriously curtailed the more egregious and rampant forms of electoral corruption in the states. Nevertheless, these reform efforts resulted in an unforeseeable side effect—they reduced the overall levels of electoral competition by stripping the once-powerful party organizations of their ability to coordinate entry decisions and encourage risk-averse candidates to run in marginally competitive races. The net result has been a dramatic increase in lopsided races, as potential quality challengers choose not to run in contests their equally situated counterparts would have 120 years ago. For the foreseeable future, then, it is difficult to imagine greater levels of electoral competitiveness becoming the norm again, especially if such reform comes with the risk of corruption at the hands of revitalized party organizations.

Notes

Chapter 1

1. Since the conclusion of the Civil War, there have only been four elections in which the president's party gained seats at the midterm: 1866, 1934, 1998, and 2002.

2. Two seats were vacant at the outset of both congresses. There were 3 seats held by third parties in the 44th Congress (Ornstein, Malbin, and Mann 2002).

3. The Australian ballot introduced the notion of privacy of candidate selection at the ballot box. Prior to its adoption in the states in the early 1890s, voting was not a private act, but was conducted publicly. As the name implies, the secret ballot was originally developed in Australia earlier in the nineteenth century.

4. One notable exception to this trend is Kolodny (1998), who documents the emergence of congressional campaign committees after the Civil War.

Chapter 2

1. For a definitive account of the politics of congressional elections in the post–World War II era, see Jacobson (2009).

2. As Kernell (1977) suggests, "Not until the adoption of the Australian ballot throughout the country in the late 1890s did many congressmen have much prospect of 'controlling' their district."

3. Recent empirical work by Ansolabehere, Hansen, Hirano, and Snyder (2010) suggests that the direct primary significantly enhanced intra-party competition in U.S. House races, but had a very limited effect on general election competitiveness.

Chapter 3

1. See Chapter 4 for a more detailed discussion of coding candidate quality.

2. Unlike modern day congressional elections where candidates often gain valuable benefits such as increased name recognition from running more than once, running and losing during the late nineteenth century most likely did not yield the same electoral benefits. For one thing, the party organizations played a much more active role in determining which candidates would run in one election to the next. This major difference in candidate selection would seem to downplay the levels of name recognition or experience that might otherwise be gained. With the parties orchestrating electoral candidacies, these individual-level factors were probably less relevant to the candidates themselves prior to the adoption of ballot reform and the emergence of the direct primary system where voters become more directly involved in the selection of individual candidates.

3. While electoral fraud was not nearly as widespread as the anti-party reformers claimed, it was an issue that resonated with the public, so "agitators" had a relatively easy time convincing state legislatures to enact reform (Fredman 1968).

4. The history of why the direct primary was adopted is fascinating, but is beyond the scope of this analysis. See Merriam and Overacker (1928) and Ware (2002) for more details.

5. For an alternative view of political amateurs' motivation for running for Congress in the modern era, see Canon (1993).

6. Kernell (2003) reconsiders the role of institutional changes at the end of the nineteenth century on the growing degree of careerism among incumbent legislators and concludes that these factors offer only a partial explanation for the emerging trends of this era.

7. Mayhew (1974) focuses primarily on the post–World War II era and is silent on the subject of whether his argument about the electoral connection applies outside of the modern era. Nevertheless, many of the institutions that Mayhew points to as facilitating legislators' reelection bids such as the committee system and the seniority norm have been around since well before World War II. This is an important factor in that it provides some basis for arguing that an electoral connection may be present across time. For a more general treatment of this subject, see Carson and Jenkins (2007).

Chapter 4

1. We chose not to focus on Senate elections during our analysis of this era since senators did not become directly elected until after 1913 when the 17th Amendment was adopted. For a general discussion of Senate elections before popular election, see Schiller and Stewart (2004); for Senate elections after direct election, see Highton (2000).

2. We recognize, of course, that these numbers are inflated given that they reflect only those incumbents that sought reelection. If all incumbents were included, the percentages would be somewhat lower given that there is variation in the proportion of incumbents who seek reelection.

3. Both 1910 and 1922 also stand out as low points for Republicans, with only about 66 percent of Republican incumbents returning to office in each of these midterm elections.

4. After the 1894 midterm elections, 1876 and 1920 stand out as the worst years for incumbent Democrats, with approximately 30 percent of incumbents seeking reelection losing in each of these elections.

5. Although some might conclude from this trend that House incumbents appear to be getting safer over the time period we analyze, we are somewhat hesitant to draw this conclusion ourselves. Indeed, this pattern could simply reflect a decline in the number of experienced challengers running against incumbents, which would make it appear as though incumbents are getting safer. We address this issue more systematically in Chapter 6.

6. Available online at:
http://bioguide.congress.gov/biosearch/biosearch.asp.

7. The Political Graveyard can be accessed at:
http://www.politicalgraveyard.com.

8. These include directories of state legislators during nearly this entire era for California, Connecticut, Indiana, Minnesota, Missouri, New York, North Carolina, Ohio, Oregon, South Carolina, Virginia, and Wisconsin.

9. On occasion, it appears that the party organizations would call upon these former members when a vacancy in the House would occur to serve for a term or two until another candidate could be recruited to run for the House seat.

10. Note that our data do not meet the limited conditions under which listwise deletion is preferable to multiple imputation (King et al. 2001, 58). We imputed the missing values using the AMELIA software

developed by Gary King, using district presidential vote, previous candidate quality in the district, previous congressional vote in the district, and the number of outlets we had searched for the candidate quality data as predictors in the imputation equation, which was set to produce a binary imputation. The distribution of imputed candidate quality varied by year and party, with an overall mean of 35 percent imputed as quality. In the data we found, the proportion of quality candidates was approximately 70 percent.

11. Parsons, Beach, and Parsons (1990) was especially useful for determining whether the population within a county represented at least 50 percent of the district's total population. In the end, the excluded districts all came from a few large urban areas (e.g., New York, Philadelphia, Chicago) where it was impossible to map county-level data onto the appropriate congressional districts. This is not optimal, as party machines were stronger in these urban areas and thus may have been more effective at recruiting quality candidates. However, much like today, many urban districts were not competitive electorally, and including these districts in models without presidential vote share as a covariate does not alter our findings on the importance of challenger quality.

12. We also examine the correlation between Democratic presidential vote and prior vote share for Democratic incumbents and find a strong correlation (above 0.8) regardless of the type of ballot employed. This suggests to us that presidential vote share is a reasonably good proxy for the underlying partisanship of the constituency, especially since it is independent of the popularity of the incumbent legislator.

13. Given the dispute over whether the shoestring ballot was actually a form of the Australian ballot we have elected to code it as a non-Australian ballot (Ware 2002). This decision does not affect any of our substantive results and is merely for parsimony.

14. Some states made the direct primary optional for parties. The data presented herein is for mandatory primary laws only.

15. Data on the adoption dates and changes in direct primary laws are taken from Merriam and Overacker (1928); Overacker (1928, 1930, 1932, 1934, 1936, 1940); and West (1914, 1915a,b, 1922, 1924, 1926).

16. For a more extensive discussion on redistricting practices during this era, see Engstrom (2006); Engstrom and Kernell (2005).

17. We are thankful to Erik Engstrom for sharing much of his redistricting data for nineteenth and early twentieth century elections.

Chapter 5

1. The Republicans controlled only 86 seats in the House following the disastrous 1890 midterm election, but this number actually reflected a greater proportion of seats for them compared to 1936 since the size of the House in 1890 was capped at 332 seats.

2. For more details on the 1938 midterm elections, see Carson (2001).

3. Note that adding in annual data on the state of the economy necessitated that we drop the year fixed-effect terms. We also fit these models for the balance of the elections in our historical elections data-set and as Lynch predicts, we found less consistent effects for the economy. When we include 1932 in the analysis we see very strong effects of economic conditions as the change in GNP for that year is by far lowest value in our data. If we omit 1932 as an outlier we find results more consistent with what Lynch hypothesizes.

4. Note that given the paucity of states adopting "open" primaries in this era and the inconsistencies in the definition of "closed" primaries, we lump both open and closed primaries together. We also omit non-mandatory primaries.

5. The standard error on these two predicted probabilities is 0.02.

6. This difference is neither statistically nor substantively significant.

7. Feasible values of lagged Democratic vote are 0 to 50 for Figure 5.1 and 50 to 100 for Figure 5.2.

8. We also estimate a single model that includes a series of interaction terms between ballot type and Democratic Quality Advantage. The results of this model were statistically and substantively indistinguishable from those reported above.

9. A Chow test reveals that coefficient estimate for Democratic Quality Advantage in the office bloc model is significantly different from the party column $(\chi^2(1) = 35.74)$ and party ballot $(\chi^2(1) = 40.62)$ specifications, but there is not a discernible difference between the party column and party ballot $(\chi^2(1) = 0.47)$. The OB-Box model is significantly different than the party ballot and party column models, but the Chow test for the OB-Box/Office Bloc comparison just misses statistical significance $(\chi^2(1) = 2.43)$.

10. Party unity is coded as the percent of party votes (pitting at least one-half of one party against one-half of the other) in which a member voted with his or her party. Competitiveness is coded as the

percentage of the two party vote received by the losing candidate in the previous election, with larger numbers reflecting more competitive seats. To insure that our results are not unduly influenced by elections occurring before either the Australian ballot or the direct primary was introduced, we restrict our cases to elections that took place after 1896. Standard errors are clustered by member. We also fit separate models for Republican and Democratic members. Republicans displayed less unity overall, but the substantive effects of the independent variables were indistinguishable across the two parties.

Chapter 6

1. We omit uncontested races from all the analyses in this book. Doing so likely decreases our estimates of the incumbency advantage, as scaring off all challengers is perhaps the greatest manifestation of the positive effects of incumbency. Our data also sees a more consistent level of uncontested races than is seen later in the twentieth century.

2. Data from 1946–2002 provided by Gary C. Jacobson. Vertical lines denote the election years 1946 and 1964.

3. We follow the convention of Cox and Katz (1996) and omit the following "regular" redistricting years: 1902, 1912, 1932, and 1942. Redistricting did not occur in 1922 and before 1902 redistricting was highly irregular.

4. One possibility is that changes in ballot and primary laws reduced competition. Roberts (2011) is currently exploring this potential explanation for the modern era.

5. As a robustness check, we also considered the possibility that the strategic entry and exit behavior of candidates could potentially bias the statistical estimates presented in Tables 6.1 and 6.2. In the context of research on congressional elections in the post–World War II era, evidence suggests that experienced candidates behave strategically in response to anticipated behavior on the part of incumbents (Jacobson and Kernell 1983). At the same time, the choice by an experienced candidate to challenge an incumbent could affect the likelihood that a legislator seeks reelection (Cox and Katz 2002; Gates and Humes 1997). Given these strategic considerations, it becomes necessary to consider how factors influencing these processes may be interrelated. If we examine these processes separately, we run the risk of model misspecification resulting from a possible selection effect. Failing to recognize that incumbents are also strategic actors can lead to potential

biases in how we estimate candidate competition and the incumbency advantage, which would call into question the results we present above (Cox and Katz 2002; Gelman and Huang 2008; Jenkins, Crespin, and Carson 2005; Katz 2008).

To help alleviate these concerns, we attempt to statistically model the strategic interaction between challengers and incumbents with a recursive strategic model developed by Bas, Signorino, and Walker (2008). This empirical model builds upon prior work by Signorino (1999), who has developed a set of discrete choice models for translating theoretical models into the appropriate statistical tests. These statistical models are derived from McKelvey and Palfrey (1995, 1998) and their work on quantal response equilibria (QRE) for extensive form games, based on random utility assumptions. With QRE, actors engaged in strategic interaction employ best responses to one another, given that they cannot always select the optimal strategy with absolute certainty. It is this degree of uncertainty that is reflected by the distribution of errors in their utilities that allow choice probabilities to be determined from strategic actions. The variables of interest for each actor in the strategic process are included as covariates in a strategic probit model to reflect their decisions in the underlying choice sets. Taken as a whole, the results of the strategic model confirm the substantive findings of our earlier estimates. Incumbents during the 1872–1944 period do not appear to be regularly driven from office by the likelihood of a strong challenger emerging. For the sake of parsimony and given the similarity with our earlier results, we do not report the results from the strategic probit model here In addition, recent work by Highton (2011) persuasively demonstrates that under any reasonable assumptions about how many incumbent retirements are in fact strategic and how these retirees would have done had they run, the Cox/Katz method of estimating the incumbency advantage is still robust.

6. The reader should note that this analysis only covers congressional elections held between 1872–1900 due to data limitations. After 1900 the number of states regularly redistricting drops significantly due to the declining influence of state party machines in the early decades of the twentieth century. Given that our estimation setup relies on states redistricting to gain leverage on the personal vote in House districts, it is critical to have a number of states regularly redistricting in order to have confidence in our ability to estimate the effects of the personal vote.

Chapter 7

1. Prior to the 1994 elections, the Democrats had controlled a majority of seats in the U.S. House since 1955 and the Senate for the same period except from 1981–1986.

References

Abramowitz, Alan I. 1991. "Incumbency, Campaign Spending, and the Decline of Competition in U.S. House Elections." *The Journal of Politics* 53(1):34–56.

Albright, Spencer D. 1942. *The American Ballot*. Washington D.C.: American Council on Public Affairs.

Alchian, Armen A., and Harold Demsetz. 1972. "Production, Information Costs, and Economic Organization." *The American Economic Review* 62(5):777–795.

Aldrich, John H. 1995. *Why Parties? The Origin and Transformation of Party Politics in America*. Chicago, IL: University of Chicago Press.

Alesina, Alberto, and Howard Rosenthal. 1989. "Partisan Cycles in Congressional Elections and the Macroeconomy." *American Political Science Review* 83:373–389.

Alford, John R., and David W. Brady. 1989. "Personal and Partisan Advantage in U.S. Congressional Elections, 1846–1986." In *Congress Reconsidered* (Lawrence Dodd, and Bruce Oppenheimer, editors), CQ Press, fourth edition.

Alford, John R., and John H. Hibbing. 1981. "Increased Incumbency Advantage in the House." *The Journal of Politics* 43(4):1042–1061.

Ansolabehere, Stephen, John Mark Hansen, Shigeo Hirano, and James M. Snyder. 2010. "More Democracy: The Direct Primary and Competition in U.S. Elections." *Studies in American Political Development* 24:190–205.

Ansolabehere, Stephen, James M. Snyder, and Charles Stewart III. 2000. "Old Voters, New Voters, and the Personal Vote: Using Redistricting to Measure the Incumbency Advantage." *American Journal of Political Science* 44(1):17–34.

Ansolabehere, Stephen, James M. Snyder, and Charles Stewart III. 2001. "Candidate Positioning in U.S. House Elections." *American Journal of Political Science* 45(1):136–159.

Banks, Jeffrey S., and D. Roderick Kiewiet. 1989. "Explaining Patterns of Competition in Congressional Elections." *American Journal of Political Science* 33(4):997–1015.

Bas, Muhammet, Curtis Signorino, and Robert Walker. 2008. "Statistical Backwards Induction: A Simple Method for Estimating Recursive Strategic Models." *Political Analysis* 16(1):21–40.

Baughman, John. 2008. "Legislation as Insurance: A Reconsideration of Ambition Theory and the Realignment of the 1850s." Presented at the 2008 History and Congress Workshop, George Washington University.

Bensel, Richard. 2004. *The American Ballot Box in the Mid-Nineteenth Century*. New York: Cambridge University Press.

Bianco, William T. 1984. "Strategic Decisions on Candidacy in U.S. Congressional Districts." *Legislative Studies Quarterly* 9:351–364.

Bianco, William T., David B. Spence, and John D. Wilkerson. 1996. "The Electoral Connection in the Early Congress: The Case of the Compensation Act of 1816." *American Journal of Political Science* 40(1):145–171.

Born, Richard. 1979. "Generational Replacement and the Growth of Incumbent Reelection Margins in the U.S. House." *American Political Science Review* 73(3):811–817.

Brady, David W., Kara Buckley, and Douglas Rivers. 1999a. "Elections and Insurance Incentives: Parties at the Turn of the Century." Presented at the 1999 Annual Meeting of the American Political Science Association.

Brady, David W., Kara Buckley, and Douglas Rivers. 1999b. "The Roots of Careerism in the U.S. House of Representatives." *Legislative Studies Quarterly* 24(3):489–510.

Brady, David W., and Bernard Grofman. 1991. "Sectional Differences in Partisan Bias and Electoral Responsiveness in U.S. House Elections, 1850–1980." *British Journal of Political Science* 21(2):247–56.

Cain, Bruce, John Ferejohn, and Morris Fiorina. 1992. *The Personal Vote: Constituency Service and Electoral Independence*. Cambridge: Harvard University Press.

Cain, Bruce, John Ferejohn, and Morris P. Fiorina. 1987. *The Personal Vote*. Cambridge: Harvard University Press.

Caldeira, Gregory A. 1987. "Public Opinion and the American Supreme

Court: FDR's Court-Packing Plan." *American Political Science Review* 81:1139–1153.

Campbell, James E. 1991. "The Presidential Surge and its Midterm Decline in Congressional Elections, 1868–1988." *Journal of Politics* 53(2):477–487.

Canon, David T. 1993. "Sacrificial Lambs or Strategic Politicians? Political Amateurs in U.S. House Elections." *American Journal of Political Science* 37:1119–1141.

Carson, Jamie L. 2001. "Electoral and Partisan Forces in the Roosevelt Era: The U.S. Congressional Elections of 1938." *Congress and the Presidency* 28(3):161–183.

Carson, Jamie L. 2005. "Strategy, Selection, and Candidate Competition in U.S. House and Senate Elections." *Journal of Politics* 67(1):1–28.

Carson, Jamie L., and Erik J. Engstrom. 2005. "Assessing the Electoral Connection: Evidence from the Early United States." *American Journal of Political Science* 49(4):746–757.

Carson, Jamie L., Erik J. Engstrom, and Jason M. Roberts. 2006. "Redistricting, Candidate Entry, and the Politics of Nineteenth-Century U.S. House Elections." *American Journal of Political Science* 50(2):283–293.

Carson, Jamie L., Erik J. Engstrom, and Jason M. Roberts. 2007. "Candidate Quality, the Personal Vote, and the Incumbency Advantage in Congress." *American Political Science Review* 101(2):289–301.

Carson, Jamie L., and Jeffery A. Jenkins. 2007. "Examining the Electoral Connection Across Time." *Annual Review of Political Science* 14:25–46.

Carson, Jamie L., and Stephen Pettigrew. 2011. "Strategic Politicians, Partisan Roll Calls, and the Tea Party: Evaluating the 2010 Midterm Elections." Presented at the 2011 Annual Meeting of the Midwest Political Science Association.

Carson, Jamie L., and Jason M. Roberts. 2005. "Strategic Politicians and U.S. House Elections, 1874–1914." *Journal of Politics* 67(2):474–496.

Cherny, Robert W. 1997. *American Politics in the Gilded Age, 1868–1900*. Wheeling: Harlan Davidson, Inc.

Coase, Ronald. 1937. "The Nature of the Firm." *Economica* 4:386–405.

Cover, Albert D. 1977. "One Good Term Deserves Another: The Advantage of Incumbency in Congressional Elections." *American Journal of Political Science* 21(3):523–541.

Cover, Albert D., and Bruce S. Brumberg. 1982. "Baby Books and Ballots: The Impact of Congressional Mail on Constituency Opinion." *American Political Science Review* 76(3):347–359.

Cox, Gary W., and Jonathan N. Katz. 1996. "Why Did the Incumbency Advantage in U.S. House Elections Grow?" *American Journal of Political Science* 40(2):478–497.

Cox, Gary W., and Jonathan N. Katz. 2002. *Elbridge Gerry's Salamander: The Electoral Conseqences of the Reapportionment Revolution.* Cambridge: Cambridge University Press.

Cox, Gary W., and Mathew D. McCubbins. 1993. *Legislative Leviathan: Party Government in the House.* Berkeley, CA: University of California Press.

Cox, Gary W., and Mathew D. McCubbins. 2005. *Setting the Agenda: Responsible Party Government in the U.S. House of Representatives.* Cambridge: Cambridge University Press.

Dallinger, Fredrick W. 1897. *Nomination for Elective Office.* Harvard Historical Studies.

Dubin, Michael J. 1998. *United States Congressional Elections, 1788–1997: The Official Results of the Elections of the 1st Through 105th Congresses.* Jefferson: McFarland and Company.

Engstrom, Erik J. 2006. "Stacking the States, Stacking the Nation: The Partisan Consequences of Redistricting in the 19th Century." *American Political Science Review* 100(3):419–427.

Engstrom, Erik J., and Samuel Kernell. 2005. "Manufactured Responsiveness: The Impact of State Electoral Laws on Unified Party Control of the Presidency and U.S. House of Representatives, 1840–1940." *American Journal of Political Science* 49(3):547–565.

Engstrom, Erik J., and Jason M. Roberts. 2009. "The Politics of Institutional Choice: Evidence from Ballot Laws." Presented at the 2009 Annual Meeting of the American Political Science Association.

Erikson, Robert S. 1971. "The Advantage of Incumbency in Congressional Elections." *Polity* 3(3):395–405.

Erikson, Robert S. 1972. "Malapportionment, Gerrymandering, and Party Fortunes." *American Political Science Review* 66(4):1234–1245.

Erikson, Robert S. 1990. "Economic Conditions and the Congressional Vote: A Review of the Macrolevel Evidence." *American Journal of Political Science* 34:373–399.

Evans, Eldon Cobb. 1917. *A History of the Australian Ballot in the United States.* Chicago: University of Chicago Press.

Fenno, Richard F. 1978. *Home Style: House Members in Their Districts*. New York: Longman.

Ferejohn, John A. 1977. "On the Decline of Competition in Congressional Elections." *American Political Science Review* 71(1):166–176.

Finocchiaro, Charles J., and David W. Rohde. 2008. "War for the Floor: Partisan Theory and Agenda Control in the U.S. House of Representatives." *Legislative Studies Quarterly* 33:35–62.

Fiorina, Morris P. 1977. "The Case of the Vanishing Marginals: The Bureaucracy Did It." *American Political Science Review* 71(1):177–181.

Fiorina, Morris P. 1989. *Congress: Keystone of the Washington Establishment*. New Haven: Yale University Press, second edition.

Fiorina, Morris P., David W. Rohde, and Peter Wissel. 1975. "Historical Change in House Turnover." In *Congress in Change* (Norman J. Ornstein, editor), New York: Praeger Publishers, pp. 24–57.

Fredman, L.E. 1968. *The Australian Ballot: The Story of an American Reform*. East Lansing: Michigan State University Press.

Gaddie, Ronald K., and Charles S. Bullock. 2000. *Elections to Open Seats in the U.S. House: Where the Action Is*. New York: Rowman and Littlefield Publishers.

Garand, James C., and Donald A. Gross. 1984. "Changes in the Vote Margins for Congressional Candidates: A Specification of Historical Trends." *American Political Science Review* 78(1):17–30.

Gates, Scott, and Brian D. Humes. 1997. *Games, Information and Politics: Applying Game Theoretic Models to Political Science*. University of Michigan Press.

Gelman, Andrew, and Zaiying Huang. 2008. "Estimating Incumbency Advantage and Its Variation, as an Example of a Before-After Study." *Journal of the American Statistical Association* 103:437–446.

Gelman, Andrew, and Gary King. 1990. "Estimating Incumbency Advantage Without Bias." *American Journal of Political Science* 34(4):1142–1164.

Groseclose, Timothy, and Keith Krehbiel. 1994. "Golden Parachutes, Rubber Checks, and Strategic Retirements from the 102d House." *American Journal of Political Science* 38(1):78–99.

Highton, Benjamin. 2000. "Senate Elections in the United States, 1920–94." *British Journal of Political Science* 30:483–506.

Highton, Benjamin. 2011. "The Influence of Strategic Retirement on the Incumbency Advantage in U.S. House Elections." *Journal of Theoretical Politics* 23:431–447.

Hirano, Shigeo. 2008. "Third Parties, Elections, and Roll Call Votes in the Late Nineteenth-Century U.S. Congress." *Legislative Studies Quarterly* 33:131–170.

Jacobson, Gary C. 1987. "The Marginals Never Vanished: Incumbency and Competition in Elections to the U.S. House of Representatives, 1952–1982." *American Journal of Political Science* 31(1):126–141.

Jacobson, Gary C. 1989. "Strategic Politicians and the Dynamics of U.S. House Elections, 1946–1986." *American Political Science Review* 83(3):773–93.

Jacobson, Gary C. 1990. *The Electoral Origins of Divided Government: Competition in U.S. House Elections, 1946–1988*. Boulder: Westview Press.

Jacobson, Gary C. 1996. "The 1994 House Elections in Perspective." *Political Science Quarterly* 111(2):203–223.

Jacobson, Gary C. 2008. *A Divider, Not a Uniter: George W. Bush and the American People*. New York: Pearson Longman.

Jacobson, Gary C. 2009. *The Politics of Congressional Elections*. New York: Longman, 7th edition.

Jacobson, Gary C., and Michael A. Dimock. 1994. "Checking Out: The Effects of Bank Overdrafts on the 1992 House Elections." *American Journal of Political Science* 38(3):601–624.

Jacobson, Gary C., and Samuel Kernell. 1983. *Strategy and Choice in Congressional Elections*. New Haven: Yale University Press, second edition.

Jenkins, Jeffery A., Michael Crespin, and Jamie L. Carson. 2005. "Parties as Procedural Coalitions: An Examination of Differing Career Tracks." *Legislative Studies Quarterly* 30:365–389.

Johannes, John R., and John C. McAdams. 1981. "The Congressional Incumbency Effect: Is It Casework, Policy Compatibility, or Something Else?" *American Journal of Political Science* 25(3):520–542.

Josephson, Matthew. 1938. *The Politicos, 1865–1896*. New York: Harcourt, Brace, and Company.

Katz, Jonathan N. 2008. "Comment: Estimating Incumbency Advantage and Its Variation, as an Example of a Before-After Study." *Journal of the American Statistical Association* 103:446–447.

Katz, Jonathan N., and Brian R. Sala. 1996. "Careerism, Committee Assignments, and the Electoral Connection." *American Political Science Review* 90(1):21–33.

Kernell, Samuel. 1977. "Toward Understanding 19th Century Congressional Careers: Ambition, Competition, and Rotation." *American*

Journal of Political Science 21(4):669–693.

Kernell, Samuel. 2003. "To Stay, To Quit or To Move Up: Explaining the Growth of Careerism in the House of Representatives, 1878–1940." Presented at the 2003 Annual Meeting of American Political Science Association.

King, Gary, James Honaker, Anne Joseph, and Kenneth Scheve. 2001. "Analyzing Incomplete Political Science Data: An Alternative Algorithm for Multiple Imputation." *American Political Science Review* 95(1):49–70.

Kleppner, Paul. 1983. "Voters and Parties in the West, 1876–1900." *Western Historical Quarterly* 14(1):49–68.

Kleppner, Paul. 1987. *Continuity and Change in Electoral Politics, 1893–1928*. New York: Greenwood Press.

Kolodny, Robin. 1998. *Pursuing Majorities: Congressional Campaign Committees in American Politics*. Norman: University of Oklahoma Press.

Kramer, Gerald. 1971. "Short-term Fluctuations in U.S. Voting Behavior, 1896–1964." *American Political Science Review* 65:131–143.

Krasno, Jonathan S. 1994. *Challengers, Competition, and Reelection: Comparing Senate and House Elections*. New Haven: Yale University Press.

Ludington, Arthur C. 1911. *American Ballot Laws, 1888–1910*. University of the State of New York: New York State Education Department, Bulletin 488.

Lynch, Patrick G. 2002. "Midterm Elections and Economic Flucuations: The Response of Voters Over Time." *Legislative Studies Quarterly* 27(2):265–294.

Martis, Kenneth C. 1982. *The Historical Atlas of United States Congressional Districts, 1789–1983*. New York: Free Press.

Martis, Kenneth C. 1989. *The Historical Atlas of Political Parties in the United States, 1789–1989*. New York: MacMillan.

Mayer, Thomas, and Monojit Chatterji. 1985. "Political Shocks and Investment: Some Evidence from the 1930s." *Journal of Economic History* 45:913–924.

Mayhew, David R. 1974. *Congress: The Electoral Connection*. New Haven: Yale University Press.

Mayhew, David R. 2000. "Electoral Realignments." *Annual Review of Political Science* 3:449–474.

McKelvey, Richard D., and Thomas R. Palfrey. 1995. "Quantal Response Equilibria in Games." *Games and Economic Behavior* 10:6–

38.

McKelvey, Richard D., and Thomas R. Palfrey. 1998. "Quantal Response Equilibria for Extensive Form Games." *Experimental Economics* 1(1):9–41.

Merriam, Charles E., and Louise Overacker. 1928. *Primary Elections.* Chicago: University of Chicago Press.

Milkis, Sidney M. 1993. *The President and the Parties: The Transformation of the American Party System Since the New Deal.* Oxford: Oxford University Press.

Oppenheimer, Bruce, Richard Waterman, and James A. Stimson. 1986. "Interpreting Congressional Elections: The Exposure Thesis." *Legislative Studies Quarterly* 11:227–247.

Ornstein, Norman J., Michael J. Malbin, and Thomas E. Mann. 2002. *Vital Statistics on Congress, 2001–2002.* Washington, DC: AEI Press.

Ostrogorski, Moisei. 1964. *Democracy and the Organization of Political Parties*, volume 2. New Brunswick: Transaction Books.

Overacker, Louise. 1928. "Primary Election Legislation in 1926–27." *The American Political Science Review* 22(2):353–361.

Overacker, Louise. 1930. "Direct Primary Legislation in 1928–1929." *The American Political Science Review* 24(2):370–380.

Overacker, Louise. 1932. "Direct Primary Legislation in 1930–31." *The American Political Science Review* 26(2):294–300.

Overacker, Louise. 1934. "Direct Primary Legislation in 1932–33." *The American Political Science Review* 28(2):265–270.

Overacker, Louise. 1936. "Direct Primary Legislation in 1934–35." *The American Political Science Review* 30(2):279–285.

Overacker, Louise. 1940. "Direct Primary Legislation, 1936–1939." *The American Political Science Review* 34(3):499–506.

Peters, John G., and Susan Welch. 1980. "The Effects of Charges of Corruption on Voting Behavior in Congressional Elections." *American Political Science Review* 74:697–708.

Polsby, Nelson. 1968. "The Institutionalization of the U.S. House of Representatives." *American Political Science Review* 62(1):144–168.

Poole, Keith T., and Howard Rosenthal. 1997. *Congress: A Political-Economic History of Roll Call Voting.* Oxford University Press.

Price, H. Douglas. 1975. "Congress and the Evolution of Legislative 'Professionalism'." In *Congress in Change: Evolution and Reform* (Norman J. Ornstein, editor), New York: Praeger Publishers, Inc., pp. 2–23.

Prior, Markus. 2007. "The Incumbent in the Living Room: The Rise of Television and the Incumbency Advantage in U.S. House Elections." *Journal of Politics* 68(3):657–673.

Reynolds, John F. 2006. *The Demise of the American Convention System, 1880–1911*. New York: Cambridge University Press.

Reynolds, John F., and Richard L. McCormick. 1986. "Outlawing 'Treachery': Split Tickets and Ballot Laws in New York and New Jersey, 1880–1910." *The Journal of American History* 72(4):835–858.

Roberts, Jason M. 2011. "Ballot Laws and the Incumbency Advantage in Congress." Typescript, University of North Carolina.

Rohde, David W. 1979. "Risk-Bearing and Progressive Ambition: The Case of Members of the United States House of Representatives." *American Journal of Political Science* 23(1):1–26.

Rohde, David W. 1991. *Parties and Leaders in the Postreform House*. Chicago, IL: University of Chicago Press.

Rosenstone, Steven, and John Mark Hansen. 1993. *Mobilization, Participation, and Democracy in America*. New York: MacMillan.

Rusk, Jerrold G. 1970. "The Effect of the Australian Ballot Reform on Split Ticket Voting: 1876–1908." *American Political Science Review* 64(4):1220–1238.

Schiller, Wendy, and Charles Stewart III. 2004. "U.S. Senate Elections before 1914." Presented at the 2004 Annual Meeting of the Midwest Political Science Association.

Schlesinger, Joseph. 1966. *Ambition and Politics: Political Careers in the United States*. Chicago: Rand McNally and Co.

Signorino, Curtis. 1999. "Strategic Interaction and the Statistical Analysis of International Conflict." *American Political Science Review* 93:279–297.

Silbey, Joel H. 1991. *The American Political Nation, 1838–1893*. Palo Alto: Stanford University Press.

Stanwood, Edward. 1903. *American Tariff Controversies in the Nineteenth Century*. Houghton Mifflin.

Stewart, Charles III. 1989. *Budget Reform Politics: The Design of the Appropriations Process in the House of Representatives, 1865–1921*. New York: Cambridge University Press.

Stigler, George. 1973. "General National Economic Conditions and National Elections." *American Economic Review* 63:160–167.

Stonecash, Jeffery. 2008. *Reassessing the Incumbency Effect*. New York: Cambridge University Press.

Struble, Robert. 1979. "House Turnover and the Principle of Rotation."

Political Science Quarterly 94(4):649–667.

Summers, Mark Wahlgren. 2004. *Party Games: Getting, Keeping, and Using Power in Gilded Age Politics.* Chapel Hill: University of North Carolina Press.

Swenson, Peter. 1982. "The Influence of Recruitment on the Structure of Power in the U.S. House of Representatives, 1870–1940." *Legislative Studies Quarterly* 7(1):7–36.

Swift, Elaine L., and David W. Brady. 1994. "Common Ground: History and Theories of American Politics." In *The Dynamics of American Politics: Approaches and Interpretations* (Lawrence C. Dodd and Calvin Jillson, editors), Boulder: Westview Press, pp. 83–104.

Ware, Alan. 2002. *The American Direct Primary: Party Institutionalization and Transformation in the North.* New York: Cambridge University Press.

Welch, Susan, and John R. Hibbing. 1997. "The Effects of Charges of Corruption on Voting Behavior in Congressional Elections, 1982–1990." *The Journal of Politics* 59:226–239.

West, Victor J. 1914. "Legislation of 1913 Affecting Nominations and Elections." *The American Political Science Review* 8(3):437–442.

West, Victor J. 1915a. "Legislation of 1914 Affecting Nominations and Elections." *The American Political Science Review* 9(4):738–743.

West, Victor J. 1915b. "Legislation of 1915 Concerning Nominations and Elections." *The American Political Science Review* 9(4):743–748.

West, Victor J. 1922. "1921 Legislation Respecting Elections." *The American Political Science Review* 16(3):460–465.

West, Victor J. 1924. "Changes in Election Laws, 1922–23." *The American Political Science Review* 18(2):312–320.

West, Victor J. 1926. "Election Legislation in 1924 and 1925." *The American Political Science Review* 20(2):339–346.

Wrighton, Mark J., and Peverill Squire. 1997. "Uncontested Seats and Electoral Competition for the U.S. House of Representatives Over Time." *The Journal of Politics* 59:452–468.

Index